To Nancy ♡
Always be #EXTRA

RIDE THE WAVES & SHARE YOUR STORY.

#EXTRA Ordinary

CARLEEN MATTS-BEHRENDS

LISA SHAFFNER SOHN

WISE Ink
CREATIVE ★ PUBLISHING

D1568625

Love, Carleen + Lisa

ISBN: 978-1-63489-232-2
Library of Congress Catalog Number 2019939487

Printed in the United States of America
First Printing: 2019

23 22 21 20 19   5 4 3 2 1

Cover Design by Athena Currier
Interior Design by Kim Morehead

Wise Ink Creative Publishing
807 Broadway St. NE, Suite 46
Minneapolis, MN 55413
www.wiseink.com

Contents

Blessing • vii

Blessing

You are here to make beautiful waves in this world.

Shine your beautiful light, child.

Foreword and Stuff

Foreword and Stuff

INTRODUCTION

So, we decided to write a book.

When you take on a project like this (especially if it's your first foray into the whole book-writing thing), the enormity of the task sometimes feels like a pregnant elephant riding around in a very large Baby Bjorn strapped to your body. Even if you have people to help you carry the load, like we did, a pregnant elephant is still, nonetheless, a pregnant elephant.

There is also a bit of anxiety that comes up about what to put down on paper. Will our stories be entertaining enough? Will we move or inspire anyone? Will we have something new to say that hasn't already been said? Will everything make sense, or do we live in some alternate universe where what we say sounds like complete nonsense to everyone else but each other? What if we make mistakes? What if we say too much? What if we don't say enough? What if we step on important toes? What if we offend someone? What if people hate our sense of humor? What if we swear too much? What if this is the most epic fail ever committed by a couple of women who thought that they could pull off something this big?

After all, by societal standards, we're pretty average. We're teachers. We're moms. We're middle-aged women who need to know where the nearest bathroom is at all times. (TMI? See? We don't know! We're new at this, darn it!)

Here's the deal. We are hoping that the fact that we are pretty average teachers/moms/middle-aged women who need to know where the nearest bathroom is at all times is exactly **WHY** you're going to want to read our book.

On the boat with my bestie Kerri, my niece/ little sister Amy, my puppydog, Jussi, and my Diet Coke. (#Lini)

Me Extraño: I Miss Myself!

Carleen: One day, I was trying to be all #FanGirl and say, "I'm EXTRA" in Spanish (hablo un poco de español). I thought I'd give it a try since you teach Spanish. Turns out that "Me extraño" means, "I miss myself!" And then I realized that the Universe was nudging us (and our readers!) to rediscover the selves we've been missing. Puts a whole new spin on this book thing, doesn't it?

Lisa: EVEN BETTER! WHERE DID THOSE LLAMICLES GO???

Driving to Bismarck for the ND State swim meet our senior year. (#Lili)

We aren't celebrities with tons of money to pay for the latest procedures, and we don't have perfect houses and perfect yards and perfect children and perfect spouses. We have mortgages and credit card debt and school loans. We sometimes eat too much whiskey fudge and have one too many Jameson Gingers. Our eyeliner runs down our faces by lunchtime, and we still can't believe that no one tells us when it does. Our "natural highlights" start showing much too soon after we get our hair colored, and we can't figure out if we should go lighter or darker next time. We sometimes forget to close the garage door at night, and we lose our keys on a regular basis. Like, most days.

In short, we've been through some stuff, we've taken some rough falls, and we do NOT have everything figured out. But here's what we know for sure (Oprah can't be the only one who gets to say that, right?) (love you, Oprah!):

> We are strong,
> we are beautiful,
> we are badass, and
> we have something to SAY!

We are ordinary women with a passion for the extraordinary. In fact, we're #EXTRAordinary.

AND SO ARE YOU.

Maybe you talk a lot, like we do, or maybe you have kept your voice quietly buried under your insecurities, your responsibilities, and the expectations of everyone else in the world but yours. (We've done that too. Sometimes we still do, at least until we snap ourselves and each other out of it.)

Guess what, sisters? That time can be over if you'd like it to be. Just because we're in a certain season of life does NOT mean we are forgettable. Just because we are no longer part of the younger generation does not mean that our worth is diminished. Far from it. We are just getting started in all our perfect imperfection, and we want to invite you out to the lake.

So, grab your beachy clothings (stop it with the self critique—you're badass and gorgeous—own it!), put down whatever it is you think you need to do (it can wait!), and come with us. It's time to discover, uncover, and reacquaint yourself with . . . your SELF. She's waiting for you! WE are waiting for you!

#BeEXTRA!

BFF,
Lisa and Carleen <3

AN #**EXTRA**ORDINARY FORE**WORDCLOUD**

Apparently when you are an unknown author, a foreword is a good thing to have to bring credibility to your book. Basically, someone who is an expert in your field or is a well-known celebrity speaks up and answers the question, "Why the heck should I read this book, anyway?"

The thing is . . . we Minnesota Girls don't know any celebrities, really. And it feels a little weird to reach out to someone like Oprah or Michelle Obama completely out of the blue and say, "We love you. By the way, will you write our foreword?"

However—we DO know some experts about the topic of Women in the Middle: our family and friends who are living the good life, one day at a time. We decided to ask them to say a thing or two about aging, as well as the people who love them just the way they are. Theirs are voices we want to amplify, and theirs is wisdom we want to share so you, the reader, will know that you are in good company as you sit down to read *#EXTRAOrdinary.*

Because *#EO* is not a traditional book, we thought it really shouldn't have a traditional foreword #BecauseOfCourseItShouldnt. Right? Right. SO, we created a foreWORDCLOUD instead! #BecauseWhyNot?

If you are unfamiliar with word clouds, here's how they work. You collect some text (in this case, from a Google Form we sent out) and feed it into a word cloud generator. The image that comes out is a visual representation not only of the ideas but also of the evidence of shared ideas. The words that appear bigger are words that showed up multiple times. The bigger the word, the more people shared the idea.

The first question we asked was this: What do you think of when you contemplate aging and

being middle-aged? Here's what our experts said, in visual form:

The second question we asked was this: What are the best qualities of those who support you the most and love you just the way you are? Here's what they said:

And there you have it. <3

We'd like to thank the following expert Women in the Middle for helping us with this crazy idea of ours: Jacqueline Taradash-Bennett, Chris Kramer, Kara Gjerde, Erin Pietsch, Melissa Doerscher, Karla Smart-Morstad, Becky Mitchell, Jennifer Justen, Elizabeth Claeys, Mary Reynolds, Laura Aase, Diana Beutner, Rhiannon Nelson, Yvonne Bickerstaff, Jane Martin, Mridula Raghunathan, Alison Kenda, Mari Dailey, Sandy Homb, Kathy Seppala, Leanne Kampfe, Melanie Randall, Roxanne Johnson, Michelle Cunningham, Michelle Shaffner, Denelle Wallace-Alexander, Ann Marie Papas, Staci Lautigar, Allison Nahr, Kari Larson, Rebecca Jones, Corey Halls, Denise Swanson, Amy Gebhardt, Andrea Sebenaler, Nancy Johnson, Coreen Ball, Amy Kodet, Kathy Osborne, Kris Heimes (aka Cissy), and Dawn Hansen.

While we wish we could reprint your incredible wisdom word for word, we hope that all of you will consider sharing your stories and amplifying the voices of the WITM around you. We love you all and are glad you came along for the ride.

We ran around the Mall of America in our get-ups one Saturday, filming scenes for our Indigogo campaign video. A #LittleSister gave us the cutest little pink butterfly ring to share. #Highlight #TreasureThatIsWhatYouAre

Foreword and Stuff

#EXTRA EXPLAINED

Carleen: One thing we should explain is how the word #EXTRA became our thing. My teenager—even though he is the best thing ever—is not above rolling his eyes at me. I mean, he loves me, but sometimes I am a little much, even for him.

Now, he's a nice kid, so after some crazy thing I did (or said or wore or SOMETHING), he politely explained, "Mom . . . that's what we would say is . . . extra. Over the top. Too much. You know?" (This is 2018, for those of you who are wondering. We know that by the time this book is published, calling something "extra" will be LONG gone, but whatever. That will just make it #Vintage.)

The Boy (™) on the Golden Gate Bridge. That's my heart right there. (#Lini)

I thought, yes! That's it! I love that! That's the perfect word to describe that crazy little spark that lights up everything like the Fourth of July. I shared the story with Lisa, and we started riffing about it on social media. Pretty soon we decided everyone needed to celebrate their #EXTRA. Embrace their #EXTRA. BE #EXTRA.

This will ALWAYS be my favorite Hunkabunk #BecauseFlamingos. (#Lini)

And then we realized that #EXTRA is not JUST wearing flamingo socks, rocking a llama necklace, or putting a streak of purple in your hair after the age of forty (although it very well COULD be). #EXTRA runs deeper than that—it's the WHY behind doing those things. It's the core element of your soul that you should never apologize for. And never hide. It is the positive love energy that makes you, you. It's what makes you feel most authentic and alive . . . the Fourth of July of the Smiling Soul. BAM! POW! POP! LOVE!

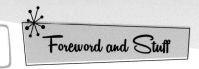
So, to the chagrin of embarrassed teens everywhere . . . we invite everyone to go forth with #EXTRA!!

Lisa: #EXTRA describes who we really are SO well! It was perfection as soon as it left the teenager's mouth! And we are so proud of our #EXTRA! Just ask us—we will tell you!

Hunkabunk + llamas = #LLAMATASTIC (#Lili)

For me, it was recently about a piece of clothing. I've got this sundress I purchased in 1986. It was lovely then, it was lovely in 1997, and it is lovely now. A few weeks ago, we were getting ready to go somewhere, and I put it on. Kiddo walks into the bathroom and says, "Mom, you need to take that off right now." My husband, Kris, walked by a minute later, took one look at me, and simply said, "No." So, I didn't wear it. I had been contemplating that scenario since that day with growing irritation. One day, I decided that not only was I going to put it on, but I was going to wear it in public! Kris wouldn't go with me, but that's okay! I rocked it at Target all by my DAMN self!

Even more recently, it was the acquisition of a llama necklace I am in love with! It is handmade by my friend, Sheri (Hunkabunk—look her up!). She is a Minot, ND (my hometown) girl and an incredibly talented artist and jeweler. This necklace is absolutely FABULOUS and all kinds of #EXTRA! She creates beautiful custom-made pieces and is now on the llama lookout for me. (The llama is quiet and awkward looking, but don't annoy her because llama kicks are highly unpleasant. Llamas will spit at you too.)

We strongly feel you need to find your #EXTRA, whatever that means to you! What is your #EXTRA? What is your spark? You don't know? Perhaps we can help you find it!

Foreword and Stuff

THE METAPHOR

Let it be known here and now that we have a thing for waterskiing. It's not that we're champion skiers by any means. (We're happy to get up on two skis these days and positively ecstatic when we are able to drop one, thank you!) No, we love it because of one particular bit of wisdom my (Carleen) big brother Cedric bestowed on me when I was a kid in the '70s.

Cedric loved to explore the world as much as I did and didn't mind if his little sister tagged along with him, at least once in a while. He knew a ton about pretty much everything—he had the kind of brain that sucked up knowledge like a Dyson. He also spent a lot of time thinking about what everything meant. He loved discussing his ideas with anyone, anywhere, although there were many people who didn't understand him because he was uber smart and marched to the beat of a different drum. I adored him, so I spent every moment I could with him. One of our favorite activities was walking through our forty acres of land in northern Minnesota. To us, it was sacred land and sacred time.

Rock hopping, we called it, or swamp slogging. Cedric went first, choosing the steadiest paths and holding back branches so I wouldn't lose an eye. He talked excitedly about whatever he thought I should know at any given moment. If he wasn't filling me with knowledge about the glaciers that scraped the rocks around us or spouting the names of every type of tree in the woods, he was educating me about complicated life lessons by using metaphors I could easily understand.

One of my favorite metaphors I have carried with me through all sorts of life adventures, both thrilling and devastating, was inspired by one of our favorite summer pastimes at the Matts family cabin on Lake Vermilion.

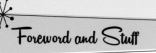

The Rules of Life, As Illustrated By Waterskiing:

1. Don't panic.
2. If you fall, fall gracefully.
3. When you fall, let go of the rope.
4. Get up and try again.

Simple words, aren't they? Simple, yet erudite. Obvious, yet subtle. Optimistic. Encouraging. A series of challenges.

The next generation—the waterskiing version! (#Lili)

The day Big Brother Kevin taught me to waterski. After a few attempts, I made it around in a circle and landed gracefully. It was a miracle. (#Lini)

I have had them posted on my classroom wall for more than twenty years—but other than an occasional, brief mention before a panic-inducing test, I haven't really thought about the depth of Cedric's metaphor until January 2018.

I was lying in bed one morning, asking myself, why do I hurt all over? Why have I had more migraines this month than I have in years? Why do I feel unrested after eight hours of sleep? Why is my old, annoying acquaintance, anxiety, insisting it deserves prime real estate in my brain these days? What is my body trying to tell me?

Then it dawned on me: I'm waterskiing through my life. But the boat is still going at full throttle, and I've got a face full of water because it's dragging me all over the bay. I haven't let go of the rope like I know I should.

I could almost hear Cedric's voice saying, "Carleen, the boat is never in control. The skier is."

Right.

This book, which uses Cedric's metaphor as its central structure, was written for a special group of women just like us: Waterskiing Women of a Certain Season of Life.

You know who you are.

There's nothing like a Lake Vermilion sunset (and it looks even more spectacular from Cedric's canoe). (#Lini)

You—like us—are the ones who chase others around (and probably have for years). We chase our kids. We chase our pets. We chase our students, if we have them. And so on, and so on, and so on.

If we're honest, we also find ourselves scrambling after people we want to impress, people we desire, people we think we need to fix, people we want to set on the right path, people we admire, and people we have no business being around because they aren't good for us (even though they might be hella cute and charming).

And if the truth serum is really flowing, we might admit we also chase versions of ourselves. We chase the versions we think other people want to know or be married to, the versions we think would be more acceptable to others, the versions that might make the pain stop because they are just a little more perfect than we are. We chase the versions that do everything right and belly laugh in the face of mistakes. We chase the versions that others may insist are better because they are younger, firmer, thinner, calmer, and cooler than we are.

Why are we so hard on ourselves when we would never speak to another human being that way? Why do we punish ourselves? Why do we deny ourselves contentedness and peace and joy and stillness? Why do we vilify aging and loathe imperfection? Why do we waste time running around in circles when we could be basking in the sun with a fruity drink—or better yet, jumping in and putting our skis on the water?

We're going to explore that metaphor in this book, girlfriends. We're going to chat about challenges and tell you our stories. We aren't going to stop there, however, and get ourselves stuck in the mud of our collective pain. You—and we—deserve so much more, and it's time we start speaking up and telling the world that we aren't done. Far from it.

We will share some of what we've learned, all in the spirit of empowering ALL of us sisters to #SpinGold out of the challenging parts of life and more fully love our beautiful, authentic selves that lie at the center of our souls and have been there since the beginning of time.

All we have to do is listen!

What if you aren't a peri/menopausal woman? What if you're a younger woman, an older woman, or even a GUY who sometimes feel like you've lost bits and pieces of yourself? Is this book for you?

YES! It most certainly is. We're going to talk about some very universal, very HUMAN experi-

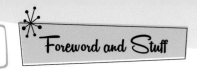

ences from all stages of life, so really, you don't need whacked-out female hormones to be a part of the team. We just feel strongly that women in the middle of life often get overlooked out there in the Wilds of the World. We wanted to write a love letter to them to say, "Hey! We see you. We hear you. We notice you. We got you. We ARE you. And Starshines, you MATTER."

So, YES, even though this book is aimed at a group you may not technically belong to, you might see yourself in here, or you might see people you love in here. Read on and see what connections you make.

Just be aware we talk about saggy boobs and extra half-asses. Not a lot, but a little. Oh, and stretch marks. There's a little bit of that in here too. But you're tough, so . . . ;)

Here's To

Here's to the crazy ones. The misfits. The rebels. The troublemakers. The round pegs in the square holes. The ones who see things differently. They're not fond of rules. And they have no respect for the status quo. You can quote them, disagree with them, glorify or vilify them. About the only thing you can't do is ignore them. Because they change things. Because the people who are crazy enough to think they can change the world, are the ones who do.

—Rob Siltanen (erroneously but understandably attributed to Steve Jobs)

Cedric at Cousin Peter's cabin on Lake Vermilion when he was in high school.

Photo Credit: Cousin Mary Heubner (#Lini)

Foreword and Stuff

A FEW WORDS ABOUT
STRUCTURE AND CIRCLES

This book is meant to be #EXTRA user-friendly! It's not sequential, like a novel, so you can jump around and take in whatever part speaks to you at any moment. You might also find yourself identifying with one of us over the other, so you may decide to read that person's stories first. Whatever works for you is golden!

One more thing to keep in mind that dawned on us as we wrote: this book is not linear, like many nonfiction books.

Self-help books typically follow a formula like this:

Step One: Meet the writer(s)
Step Two: Hear about the writer(s)' issues, challenges, and problems
Step Three: Discover what helped them
Step Four: Learn how to do what they did

The more we wrote, the more we realized our book does not follow that pattern because our lives have never been linear. And they aren't showing signs of becoming linear any time soon. We also realized this state of affairs is neither good nor bad; it just IS . . . and that's okay.

Like—you don't just get over a horrific breakup in the first 24 hours. That might take a whole lot of time, loaded nachos, angry tears, and even memento destruction (like tossing stuff down a trash shoot from three floors up) to work itself out of your system (#DontJudge). Similarly, you don't start going to the gym one day and effortlessly make it part of your normal daily routine forever. Nope. Sometimes you want to just come home from work, put on your stretchy pants, and eat half a pint of ice cream. So there. (#DontJudgeThisEitherK?).

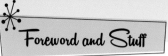

What does that mean for this book? It means that it, LIKE LIFE, will feel a little circular. We might talk about something in one part, come back around to it again in another, cross-reference the same subject again later, and so forth.

That's how our brains work. We attend to a topic, and then it floats away for a while . . . but if we aren't completely done with it, it undoubtedly reincarnates, and then we have to deal with it again.

So, rather than fight what's real in the name of appearing to have it all together (because newsflash—we don't—never have; never will), we decided to just go with it and let the soup simmer, so to speak. And when YOU sit down to write about your life and experiences, you'll do the same thing . . . but that's where the magic happens. Rome wasn't built in a day, and neither is a person's self-understanding.

THAT SAID, for those of you who would like a little map to help you get around, here's the basic structure for each section:

I. Rule of Life, As Illustrated by Waterskiing

- Letter to Our Lovelies (to get things rolling)
- Lisa Stories (because she's the big sister)
- Carleen Stories (because she's the little sister)
- Your Turn (journal questions so you can try this storytelling thing)
- #SpinGold (strategies we've tried that we want to pass along to you)

Feel free to get your own special pack of markers and write all over these pages like a textbook. Make it your own! We hope it in-

Sausage Legs

Carleen: I feel about ten pounds #EXTRA from no exercise and a sluggish digestive system. #Bullocks. It's one of those "I can't wear certain pants" kind of days.

#SurvivingSausageDays

#SausageLegsSausageFingers

#ImASausageAndEggBiscuit

#ImABigAssBowlOfHoneynutCheerios

#WhereMySugarGirlsAt

#ItsNotYourFaultItsTheSalt

#ItsJustYourAwesomePersonality TryingToBurstOuttaYourSkin

I love me some flamingo goodness, but this is pretty much my reaction to #TheBloats. (#Lini)

spires you to show your #EXTRA to the world, whatever that looks like.

Now . . . we know some of you would rather stab yourself in the eye than write in a book. We get that. If you are one of those people, you can get one of those pretty journals (or even a plain notebook). Whatever! (This would be a great hack if you are reading an electronic copy of this book.)

We just want you to know we won't be offended in the LEAST if you scribble all over our book. (We'd actually love to see pictures! In fact, it would make us cry tears of rainbows to see pictures of people and their annotated/journaled books. It's the geekiest thing about both of us as language teachers/raging empaths . . . we just LURVE us some people interacting with language.)

Here—try this little mini-journal question as a warm up! You don't have to show anyone, or you can show everyone! YOU call the shots, not the boat!

1. What kind of person are you?

- A Sharpie Person
- A Flair Pen Person
- A Gel Pen Person
- A Papermate Person
- A Colored Pencil Person
- An I-Write-With-Whatever-I-Can-Find-In-The-Couch-Cushions Person

What do you think this says about you?

_____

_____

_____

_____

_____

2. Are you someone who can write in books?

- YES! It's how I mind-meld with the ideas and the author(s). I'm like a dog marking his or her territory.
- NO! How can you even suggest writing in a beautiful book? I bet you also doggy-ear the pages, don't you, you heathen?

What do you think this says about you?

_____

_____

_____

_____

_____

All right, Girlfriends, you get the idea. Are you ready to do this? We are! Let's GO!

Rule #1

DON'T PANIC!

Chapter One

WHAT THE HELL!!

Dear Lovelies,

When it comes to life experiences, most of us fall into one of two categories of response, and the difference between them might look like this:

A. What the hell?
B. WHAT THE HELL!!

What the hell? (#WTH?) is all about having fun and trying new things that make you say, "Let's DO IT!" (like waterskiing!).

WHAT THE HELL!! (#WTH!) is a completely different thing—it's what you say when you get up in the morning, look at yourself in the mirror, and say, "This isn't right; that's not me! Where did YOU come from?"

It's maddening, isn't it?

You lean in to get a better look at the grey-hair convention popping out over your ears and temple. You study the black, puffy circles under your eyes, then rub them only to realize they exist under your skin and not ON your skin. While you're at it, you look at that age spot on your cheek (you know the one—it's located next to your adult acne) and wonder which continent it looks like today—or what disturbing image someone might see in it were it on the Rorschach test.

This is a photo of my mom, my daughter, and my Spanish daughter taking a stroll in Duluth, MN. We are all in this together and we have a lot of experience to share. (#Lili)

You turn to the side. Where did that "fluff" around your middle come from (not to mention the other fluff [or WHISKERS] on your upper lip, chin, and jawline), for Pete's sake??? When did the dimple on your butt turn into the Grand Canyon after a rock slide? What's with the furrows in your brow? Do you frown THAT much? Does it help to smile, even in a fake way? Should you get bangs . . . you know, to cover those huge forehead wrinkles? What happened to the skin under your chin? Is that a JOWL??? Why is the skin on your legs doing THAT? And what on earth happened to The Girls?

We don't know about you, but there are days when there is a complete mismatch between the seventeen-year-old spirits inside of us and the forty-something bodies they happen to live in—kind of like our own personal *Freaky Friday* without the badassery of Jamie Lee Curtis. Some days we make peace with it, but other times we avert our eyes from the mirror and dry off and dress as quickly as possible because it's too much take in. How did we let ourselves go? Why do our bodies have to age? How do we even start to make meaningful changes? Or would it just be easier to give in and eat another slice of pie? Or six (rather than have six-pack abs)?

"WHAT THE HELL!!" shows up in other parts of life, as well. Maybe it's another round of depression and anxiety, and you know you'll probably need to start on meds again, at least for a little while. Maybe it's the addiction cycle affecting your partner, your best friend, or you. Maybe it's knowing you need to get more sleep, eat better, and exercise, but you can't find the time or energy to do it. Maybe it's financial fallout from an unwise investment or home purchase. Maybe you're caught in the middle of caring for young children and aging, ill parents. Maybe it's watching your kids go through a hurtful experience you can't just kiss away. Maybe it's relationship problems. Maybe it's realizing that to be true to yourself, you might need to break off an unhealthy friendship or talk to a family member less. Maybe it's feeling like the world is falling apart—the environment, international relations, social issues, corruption—and you just don't know how you can handle it all and retain some semblance

of sanity without the help of chemicals, carbs, or retail therapy.

To make matters worse, if you don't take care of them right away, fearful thoughts have a habit of multiplying exponentially, like a cold virus with an attitude. One virus by itself is microscopic and pretty much unnoticeable. But a few million of them together can make it feel like you're trying to swallow jagged shards of glass, and it wipes you out for a few days. You can't help getting a cold once in a while, just like you can't help stressful situations from happening in your life. But just like forgetting to take our vitamin C, drink enough water, wash our hands, and get enough sleep, we sometimes find ourselves in a state of panic—the emotional equivalent of a bad, why-does-this-hurt-so-much sore throat.

So, yes. We are overly familiar with the panic thing. Yup. Lots and lots of panic between the two of us.

BFF,
Lisa and Carleen

P.S. Just so you know, we're not going to tell you our deepest, darkest secrets because we kinda just met, and we don't want to scare you away on the first date. We know that you are probably a really nice person and all, but we're just not looking to write the next big confessional book and be crowned Two Tabloid Queens With No Concept Of Boundaries Or Of How What We Say Might Hurt Others. No—we are looking to strike a balance and occupy a space where we can be personable but not overly personal. We girls need to have some secrets—they add to the mystery. We do think the stories we ARE going to tell will get our point across just fine and inspire

Gluten Sensitivity

Lisa: So, we love food. Like, all of it.

You know what's a bummer, though? We both have the gluten thing going on (yep, we're those people). Gluten sends Lisa on an extended coma-nap, and Carleen's system hates gluten AND dairy (#TRAGIC). Sometimes she plays Migraine Roulette. Like when there's . . .

Carleen: CAKE! WE LOVE CAKE! Like Nadia Cakes and NothingBundt Cake! #BestThingSinceMashedPotatoes!

Lisa: AND TACOS! WE LOVE TACOS! And #BestThingSinceMashedPotatoes?!? Allll day lonnnnnng!!!!!!

Nadia Cakes are the BEST! I had them at my wedding, and the two of us indulge in them any chance we get. (#Lini)

Rule #1

YOU to explore your own stories! After all, that's what this is all about! *SQUEEEEEEEE!!!!!!

*SQUEEEEEEEE (n): A Lisa-ism—what you say when you're REALLY JAZZED about something. If used as a question (as in, "Does this make you really jazzed?"), use just three Es ("Squeee?").

Up North

There are certain things that only those from Up North will understand. It's a common culture . . . an understanding . . . things unspoken . . . like flannels. And #LakeLife. And summer lasting 2.5 seconds. And eternal optimism. And #MNNice. And coffee 'an.
#ThatsHowWeRoll
#BrowniesAndCookiesAndCakeOhMy

Every summer Kiddo and I take the Amtrak from Union Depot in St. Paul to Minot, ND to visit Aunty Donna and Uncle Vern. This summer visit is a tradition. (#Lili)

Mom and me on the edge of Little Rice Lake, just down the road from the house where I grew up. (#Lini)

Chapter Two

Well, that Didn't Go as Planned

I always figured the first line of anything I would ever write would be: I am a firstborn, a German, a Leo, and I come from a long line of strong, independent women. It is my mantra. It is the tape that plays in my head over and over and over, always. It is what I have always taught my kiddo because she comes from that long line too. Kiddo was the first infant in the family in twenty-five years, a firstborn, an only, and an Aquarius. Our family joke (not so much a joke as it is true) is that the Appel (her Great-Great-Grandpa Walter Appel, who had a bit of a reputation for being a very stubborn and strong-willed person) didn't fall far from the tree.

For months, I had in my head that this chapter needed to be about my childhood, and then the stories and the chapters would go from there . . . wait, was that the Universe laughing at me? Why, yes, yes it was, and clearly, I did not hear it. So, I crafted incredibly witty titles of the chapters I planned to write. And then, like my actual life, it did not go AT ALL as planned! Throughout this book-writing process, I have had epiphanies, discoveries, and mind-blowing realizations. One of the main things I've realized is that my thought process isn't linear. At all. And it can't be. It can never be. Not even within the same chapter. Are you cool going on this ride with me? Great! Let's go!

I can be random and spontaneous, but I do love to control my environment. I have no desire to control others (unless they are inappropriately trying to enter my #Bubbicle), and I enjoy every person's uniqueness. That is what makes life so fun! But I do like to have a rather tight rein on who and what get to enter. Throughout the writing process, I realized that the kung-fu grip I have on the entrance to my #Bubbicle has everything to do with cushioning the fall when I inevitably wipeout.

Rule #1

Bubbicle

Lisa: Only safe people get into my inner bubbicle. If you are in my inner bubbicle, not only will I pick up the phone if you call me, but I will also pick up the phone to call you. This is huge. I'm an introvert and I hate talking on the phone.

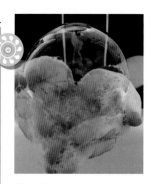

This photo was not planned. Kiddo was playing with soap while I was hiding in the bathtub. The significance of all of it, the heart shaped hands, the #bubbicle and Hamilton on her sweatshirt . . . gurl! (#Lili)

A Charmed Life

My childhood was pretty smooth. Living in Minot, ND, in the 1970s was about as wholesome as you could get. We were Lutheran. And the only diversity in town that I perceived was that there were also Catholics. Of course we had German, Norwegians, Finns, French, etc., but when I was growing up, it was perfectly acceptable to cavort with people whose grandparents came from a different country than yours. It took me a long time to realize that there were other Lutheran denominations and there was something other than Missouri Synod. I had no idea about other faiths, even though I had friends who I now know were of different faiths. When I was eighteen, my boyfriend told me he was Buddhist. I took it upon myself to write him a letter attempting to save his soul. I also took issue with him going to a Devil's music concert. Had I gone with him, I would have witnessed a very young Metallica perform their hearts out for two hours. I was very self-righteous, and now years later, very embarrassed. I have since apologized to him several times. I still can't talk about my former self-righteousness or missing that concert without cringing. He has since told me I was doing my best for him with what I had at the time, and he appreciated it. I will still forever be embarrassed. My view was narrow, and though I fancied myself a very open person, it took me time and a few huge life lessons to develop the worldview I hold today. And thank God for the Minot Air Force Base for introducing some much-needed diversity.

My childhood also consisted of days filled with "Come back for lunch" and "Be home before sundown." It was a very free and unencumbered existence. We ran around the neighborhood, in and out of each other's houses. When I got my blue ten-speed bike, I could cover much more ground in NW Minot!

Before I found freedom with my bike, I spent countless mornings walking by the Dairy Queen on 4th Avenue, passing Bee's Liquor and Oak Park Liquor (both had drive-thrus!!) before making my way to the MiniMart on 4th Ave and 16th Street. I always had a quarter so I could play PacMan before heading over to Longfellow Elementary. It was, after all, the advent of

video games. If I was lucky, Mom and Dad gave me extra money to get Corn Nuts.

Whelp . . . I'm not really sure what's going on here in my awkward 5th grade class picture. I glowed up? (#Lili)

Other childhood highlights include getting bread from Sweetheart Bakery (whose bread bags ended up inside our winter Moon Boots). I still remember the smell of baking bread, and I still have the political Charlie Brown stickers they put inside the bags in the mid-70s! They were the days of John Prine, Xanadu, and the Oak Ridge Boys on the eight-track during long car trips. Bazooka gum, Pop Rocks, and Archie Comics. Roller skates, TigerBeat, and Leif Garrett (GAWD, he was HOT!). Discovering FM radio and lying next to Mom and Dad's stereo every Friday night and Sunday after church listening and listening and listening! That's when I fell in love with Journey, Billy Joel, Toto, and The Clash. I spent countless hours taping songs from the radio and trying to end the recording at just the right time so the DJ wouldn't cut in. I spent hours rewinding cassette tapes and writing down lyrics so I could sing along. We had long, cold winters and never-ending summers. It was everything a kid could ask for. I was completely unaware not every family was like mine. In fact, once I got into high school, I was shocked at the number friends who did not have a similar family/life dynamic.

I was a relatively cute kid, and I was completely unaware of my chubby, cringey stage (grades three to six) until much later. My fifth-grade school photo did not get funny until just a few years ago. Although I can laugh at it now, I couldn't for a really really long time. So, when I was chubby as a child, I didn't know it. And when I wasn't fat at all, I thought I was. Unfortunately we were all pretty good at self-deprecating terms like fatty fatty two-by-four, thunder thighs, tundra hog, and lunar swinus (credit to Amy G. for lunar swinus). And what 80's girl could forget Bender's line to Claire in *The Breakfast Club*, "Well, not at present, but I could really see you pushing maximum density." Pushing maximum density was not something any of us wanted. Because how would we EVER fit into our pinstripe Zena jeans?

Some of my childhood obliviousness was my personality, but some was due to the dependability of my stable home. It was filled with routine and peace 99.9 percent of the time. My parents never fought, except for one time that I can recall. They play fought at times, with my mom occasionally flipping my dad off. What made it funny was she did it wrong. What made it even funnier was that for a while she didn't realize it.

Because of this home environment, our conflicts always got resolved. We were raised in an

atmosphere of absolute and unconditional love. If we hit each other, we knew Mom or Dad would open a can of whoop ass. One look from Dad and it was OVER.

At home I asserted myself, but in public I was so shy and quiet. I worked hard to not stand out. It was palpable and painful. If I didn't know you, I wouldn't talk to or look at you unless I absolutely had to. At parent teacher conferences, it was always the same story: she is so quiet, so shy. Any panic I felt was directly related to unwanted attention. If the spotlight was on me, I felt like I was going to die. I didn't want anyone to look at me. Ever. It had nothing to do with my appearance. I have no idea what it was about, but there are at least three photos of me in public situations where I cannot look at my shoes hard enough. And smile? No way! Not. Gonna. Happen. I was too busy dying of embarrassment.

There was a time in grade school when I hid from a neighbor boy because of my propensity for embarrassment. We went to school together. We were in the same class. When we were seven, he spent hours teaching me how to ride my bike in the shared alley behind our houses. But on one occasion, I had a horrific moment of thinking he was cute (he was). So when I saw Nathan coming down the alley and he saw me, I panicked (omg, I panicked), ran to my parent's car, GOT IN, and hid on the floor boards. He. Could. See. Me. He asked me what I was doing, and I had no answer. I just waited for him to get bored and go away. Smooth move, Ex-lax. This is probably why he didn't talk to me in high school.

I grew into a woman with an immense amount of stubborn German orneriness (that at times borders on oppositional defiance) and Norwegian confidence. Quiet confidence. Brick-wall confidence. I have frustrated more than one person in my life. Not sorry. The women I looked up to were tough as nails and they modeled that 24/7. They did no harm and took no shit. That was my normal. The women on all sides of my family really are the nicest people until you make us mad. I didn't come into my own (because I was busy looking at my shoes) until I was in my teens, but when that little piece of my #EXTRA rolled in, it was fierce and immobile.

Emerging from My Shell

My parents were both well-loved and well-respected teachers in the school district. Mom taught first grade at McKinley, and Dad taught just about every subject during his tenure at St. Leo's, Minot Air Force Base, and Erik Ramstad Junior High.

Dad had been teaching at Ramstad for a year before my class got there. It was pretty cool to be in the same building as him. I think it helped me come out of my seventh-grade shell a little

bit, and it gave me some social capital. Nearly everyone loved having him as their teacher. But I never got placed in his class. I think one of the best things about having him there, though, is that he kept me out of trouble. Not that I was a troublemaker, but if there was ever a time that I acted like a jerk, eighth grade was it. The problem was that Dad found out anything I was planning to do before I could even do it because my classmates ratted me out! Eventually I gave up on the naughty things, and did silly things like walk like a penguin when coming back from lunch to see if I could get a laugh from anyone. And that is probably where my love of making people laugh started! I figure out any possible way to put a humorous spin on anything. If I can brighten someone's day, I feel like I've done my civic duty.

Strawberry Lake

I was in sixth grade when we bought the cabin at Strawberry Lake. It needed a lot of work, as it had been uninhabited for thirty years. But we did the work and I am so proud to have been a part of it.

Dad bought a boat the first summer we owned it. The little green fishing boat represented freedom. It was so little, but that didn't matter. I could motor myself to the middle of the lake and sit there in abject, blissful peace. Strawberry Lake is small, so if my mom needed me back, all she had to do was holler and I heard her no matter where I was. But while I was out there, nothing and nobody ELSE could get at me. #Bubbicle. Perfection!

By the time I was in high school, we had a speedboat. I found friends whose families also had cabins on the lake. We drank because of course we did. We tried chewing tobacco. We swore. We found my friend's brother's girly magazines. We got 25-cent candy at the little store. We watched out for Nina in her El Camina (Camino doesn't rhyme with Nina) because she might yell at us. We drove with three people on three-wheelers. Nina's yelling? Legit. We tubed and skied all.the.time. The best thing was running that boat at full throt-

Strawberry Lake, a.k.a. Lisa's Happy Place. (#Lili)

tle and feeling the wind whipping through my (permed) hair. It was like flying! The other best thing was watching my dad try to flip my friends off the tube! He also taught them to ski. And I think he taught most of them to relax.

We had countless campfires and Dad would play guitar and sing. He sang John Denver and

John Prine. And I got lost in song and was mesmerized by the beauty of the dancing flames. And I still do.

My earliest memories of campfires include camping up at Moose Mountain in Saskatchewan, which was my very first happy place. The smell of the air is indescribable. So dreamy and relaxing! Campfires have been a constant throughout my life. A campfire would never be complete without my dad playing guitar and singing, s'mores, and Tonkas. What is a Tonka? Well, let me tell you!

Delicious! That is all. (#Lili)

Tonkas are God's gift to people who love pizza, pie, and campfires. You make a Tonka using a cast-iron clam shell on the end of two long, wooden sticks. You open up the clamshell, butter two pieces of very thin white bread, place the butter side down on each of the clam shell halves, and spoon filling onto one of the pieces of bread. We usually make pizza, apple, or blueberry Tonkas. When you fill them, make sure you don't spoon too much on the bread—otherwise it won't bake correctly. Close the clam, trim the excess bread off the outside, and set it in the hot coals. Once it's done, you have a hot and perfect pie! But be careful! The fruit pies are exceedingly hot, and if you're not careful, you will burn the crap out of your tongue!

The lake years were filled with endless summer nights (well, they WERE endless) and lazy, hot summer days spent with sunflower seeds, ice-cold Diet Coke, and my best friends and me lying out in the boat in the middle of the lake. Summer literally lasted f-o-r-e-v-e-r. The friendships, my family, the good times! The smell of Finesse shampoo instantly brings me back to the days spent at the lake. Cue "Summer of '69," "Summer Nights," and "Glory Days"! My happy place is on the water . . . any water . . . because of all of this. Or maybe it was always in me, and I got lucky that I have always been able to get myself near water. And some nights, if we were really lucky, we would get to see a beautiful show of the northern lights. It was incredibly magical. A happy place. And a happy place is indispensable. Everyone needs a happy place.

I was also fortunate enough to be in a 4-H club for several years. Our club was called Sugar -n- Spice! My mom was the leader for a while, and my Grandma Bert was a leader before her. I learned so many practical and valuable things in 4-H. At the end of the day, I could cook a whole meal, and help clear vines out of a double lot. I could sew an entire outfit, and haul countless rocks down to the shoreline. I could bake a cake, and help dig a hole for septic. I could give presentations on sides of beef and semolina, and help my dad roof the cabin. I could crochet a dishcloth, and paint a deck. I could craft, and help put a dock in.

My collective childhood experiences solidified the idea that I could do anything anyone else can do, regardless of gender. I didn't even think about it; it was just something I knew. There was absolutely no doubt in my mind. Tell me I can't do something and watch me dig in my heels to prove you wrong! All these pieces helped fundamentally form who I am and how I deal with adversity.

Searching for My Team

For as introverted as I was, my relationships with people became my purpose and the center of my being. Barring the few friendships I walked away from (do no harm, but take no shit), I am extremely loyal. Once you are my friend, you are my friend forever. I wanted forever people. I still want forever people.

The only huge, panicky friend drama I ever really had centered around Dan, to whom I am eternally grateful. There is no way I could have ever known how important he would be in my life then, in my late twenties, again in my thirties, and now. He passed away several years ago. We had lost touch. The last time I saw him was in Minneapolis, New Year's Eve of 2000, at First Avenue. He was handing out flyers for upcoming shows. When I tried to call him after that night I realized that he had given me an incorrect phone number. He disappeared from my life and I never heard from him again.

Dan was this super cute, quirky, awkward kid who moved from Roseau, MN, to Minot, ND, in tenth grade. He was funny and loveable, and he only lived a few blocks away from me. He drove an amazing little Saab that sometimes started and sometimes didn't. It had a particular smell—not good or bad, just particular! In my mind, it smelled like Europe. It was exotic, and so was Dan. He was a PK (pastor's kid for all of you non-Lutherans) and he was gay. He introduced me to horror movies, Monty Python, and Bavarian cream donuts.

He came out to me when we were 16 years old. He was in our living room sitting on Mom's stationary bike, and we passed notes back and forth because he was too afraid to tell me aloud. I had zero experience with anything he was going through, but I didn't care. He was my friend, and I loved him. People asked me all the time if he was gay, and I protected him and always said no. You couldn't be gay in Minot, North Dakota, in the '80s. It was impossible. It was dangerous. He made keeping his secret hard for me, though, when he dressed in drag for Halloween. Or when he came back from California our junior year with a hot pink and white checked manpri ensemble. I worked overtime to reassure all kinds of people that, yes, Dan was absolutely straight. Straight as an arrow. The perfect image of not gay. Really, Dan? I was

trying to not get his ass kicked! I confronted him about it, and he just laughed and laughed!

What I didn't know at the time was that my experience with Dan would serve me well in the future. Several times. He is one, though, who made me panic from time to time because protecting him was a full-time job. The biggest panic came after we graduated from high school. Our mutual friend, Chuck, found out from someone else that Dan was gay. There was a tense phone call that resulted in Chuck flying down the hill to the valley, where I lived. That was when I had my first taste of advocacy for the LGBTQIA community. Chuck was a really, really big dude, and though I knew he would never hurt me, an angry and confused eighteen-year-old Chuck was totally intimidating. With his anger pasted on his face, he just listened to me. And listened some more. At the end of our conversation, Chuck decided he valued Dan's friendship too much to lose him over such a silly thing. It wasn't silly. It was a really big deal back then to be an ally. But after that initial conversation, Chuck barely even blinked. And no one was going to get in Chuck's way about it. No one got in Chuck's way about much of anything, really, because the consequences would have been very unpleasant. And he would absolutely correct you if he felt you were wrong.

Hold My Beer

One out-of-character thing for me when I was young, but then started a continuous streak of purposefully putting myself in uncomfortable situations, was when I tried out for and kept first chair clarinet throughout three years of high school. Thank you, Mrs. (Kulish) Feldner, for encouraging your shy ninth grade student! That meant a lot to me! We had a 100-piece band, and band was cool! From that I launched into #AllTheBands: pep band, jazz band, marching band, the centennial band, pit orchestra, and actual orchestra. #BandKidsRock

Having done that, though, I still don't like being the center of attention. So wait, I know! I'll be a public-school teacher. And I'll teach high school students. And I will teach Spanish, my second language. But after seven years of teaching, I quit and went to work for Wells Fargo as a communications specialist for retirement plan services (I had zero content knowledge . . . what???). I gave enrollment and investment update meetings across the country in both languages (shy and introverted . . . what the WHAT???). But I missed the classroom, interviewed in August after one year, and landed a job at a junior high (not my age group . . . whaaaaaaaa???) in the Twin Cities Metro area. And I became a union building rep. And then I moved to the high school, and eventually I became department chair. And then I started a new program where I taught concurrent enrollment upper-level Spanish courses through the University of Minnesota. And then I became the district's world language curriculum

coordinator and helped start two more new language programs. And then I presented at our National World Language Convention. Twice. And then I wrote this book. Seriously, what the HELL? How was I not in total panic at all times? The only explanation is that I'm an extroverted introvert. Odd.

I am still pretty uncomfortable in unknown situations, and I am a complete awkward llama if I am forced into a social situation with people I don't know (except for teenagers who come to learn Spanish with me. I LOVE those guys!). I can fake it, and I'm getting way better at being authentic when I'm TOTALLY not feeling it, but it is exhausting, and I can only take so much. I was the kind of kid who needed an entire hour alone after school before I could interact with anyone else. Mom had my back and always let my friends know they had to come back or call later when I was ready for people to enter my #Bubbicle. I am still this way. I can forgo daily decompressing for a short time, but if I am not paying attention and forget to attend to it, I tend to lose my cool over trivial things.

I should feel a little weird about this chapter and the fact that I don't have any truly panic-worthy stories, but I don't. Wanna know why? Because I got my ass handed to me as an adult. The universe, sporting serious side-eye, finally got sick of me having a pretty easy go of things, and said, "That's enough. Hold my beer."

Chapter Three

CARLEEN STORIES

Itchy Demon

My name is Carleen, and I am a Recovering Professional Little Sister. ("We love you, Carleen.") Thank you.

It's hard not to be one when you're an Oops Baby who shows up nine years after the thought-to-be-last kiddo of the family (my apologies to my brother Kevin, who must have thought he had the family role of "youngest child" in the bag until I came along).

In my two brothers and my sister, I had three extra parents who helped raise me while my actual parents worked hard to support our family. Each of my siblings filled my world with their own unique interests and loves that made me well-rounded, curious, and open to every sort of experience. I know now, of course, that they probably entertained me "for a season" and then gracefully passed me on to the next caretaker in the rotation. God bless them for never showing any irritation or impatience if they felt it. All I felt was sibling bliss, which I miss so much now.

Big Brother Cedric introduced me to *The Hobbit* and *Star Wars* and *The Chronicles of Narnia*, and he read these books to me with such animation, I believed I was actually right there with Bilbo, Princess Leia, and Lucy. Sometimes he amused us both by regularly challenging me to a Picture War, in which one of us would start by drawing something harmless (like a feather), and then the other person would draw something to "interrupt" the first person's thing (like Old Man Winter's breath). We'd go back and forth until we had something akin to a reverse Rube Goldberg machine. He bought me every *Star Wars* movie soundtrack and a few collections of Mozart flute sonatas. Most important, he took me on grand adventures both in

the woods and in his canoe on the lake. Whether it was a single leaf on a tree, or the rhythm of the waves on the side of the canoe, Cedric helped me see art in everything.

Big Sister Cissy (her real name is Kristin—pronounced "Kristine," but I never call her that #BecauseCissy) and I spent a lot of time in the kitchen cooking and baking (and stealing frosting from the green Tupperware bowl, which got us in trouble with Mom, who had been saving it for banana cupcakes—I now understand it was Mom's version of my present-day secret stash of chocolate chips in the back of the cupboard). Cissy was a sewing master who made me super cute clothing (I had my own private seamstress and TOTALLY didn't know how good I had it!). Almost every night, she patiently listened to me babble away as we went to sleep in twin beds in our room (eventually she'd stop responding to me, and then I'd sigh and say, "Goodnight, Cissy . . ."). She also played guitar and taught me every church youth group song imaginable, which gave me a strong foundation for my belief in the power of Love over the destruction of Fear.

Big Brother Kevin was the one who showed me how exciting it was to create something out of raw materials. He could make a junky car beautiful with putty, a sander, and an air compressor. He built gorgeous shelves and furniture out of wood. Like my other siblings, he also had a love for music. He performed in a quartet, worked as a local DJ celebrity on WHLB FM, and collected a LOT of rock and roll (the mixtape skillz he shared with me sure came in handy when I was a teenager in love in the 1980s). Kevin was a visionary, and he taught me the value of having a dream and working hard to make it happen. He also sacrificed a lot of his time and earnings to give me experiences like concerts and amusement park trips—something our parents couldn't afford to give the older three kids.

Now that I am a parent and a teacher, I know what they were doing: they were giving me the best of what they had—their special take on what made life beautiful—their #EXTRA. As a young kid without much perspective on life, I didn't thank them enough.

To add another layer, I now more fully understand they were insulating me as much as they could from the dysfunction of our house. Oh, I was well aware of the cloud of pain we were living under—I witnessed it, experienced it, and rode BIG waves of cortisol for YEARS because of it—but I made it through to adulthood a little less damaged because of the selfless love of my siblings.

But despite their protection, anxiety was still my constant companion (and still is). When I was a little girl, my mom used to say, "Carleen, don't worry so much!" Yes, it's true: I worried about EVERYTHING. Were the trees going to fall on top of the cabin during a thunderstorm and crush us all? Was my head going to get chopped off if I didn't duck when we drove under the railroad bridges stretching across the highway? What if the Wicked Witch of the West were real and hiding in my closet at night? What if no one would marry me because I couldn't fold a fitted sheet? If there was a nuclear war, would death come from a ground-zero detonation or the drawn-out torture of radiation sickness and nuclear winter?

I can laugh at Little Me now that I have a little bit of life experience behind me and know that most of those scenarios were pretty ridiculous (well, except for the nuclear war thing). But at that time, Fear had the power to hijack my sense of safety and completely paralyze me. There were times when I had absolutely no idea what to do to stop from perseverating on the Worst Case Scenario of the Day—instead, I curled up in a fetal position and waited out the beating (which never came). I also had no idea that I was the one giving Fear so much power.

Little Girl Me, safe in the company of my #EXTRAParents. Gotta dig Cedric's pants. (#Lini)

Looking back and considering what my childhood was like, I am not surprised that my Little Brain's default setting was "WORRY" because I had stress coming at me from all directions. It was the 1970s and 1980s: the Soviet Union was the reported bully down the street, gas stations were running out of fuel, and Bigfoot and the aliens were most likely conspiring to kidnap me and turn me into the latest creepy story on *Unsolved Mysteries*.

But it wasn't really the "bigger world" stuff that stressed me out the most. To be real, the bully in my life was my father—a hurting man who, despite his best but sometimes twisted efforts to be a good father, was particularly adept at hurting others. The shortage in my life was the fact our family was always struggling to pay the bills and put food on the table (usually wieners on bread and Campbell's soup). The monsters in my life were the people who I imagined dismissed me as a forgettable, awkward kid who didn't wear the right clothes and spent too much time being the teacher's pet (when really I was just more comfortable talking to adults).

To make matters even worse (or maybe as a result of all that stress), my little body, from my backside to my knees and around to the outer sides of my calves, was covered in an itchy, red rash for much of my childhood and adolescence. I just had.to.scratch. I couldn't help it. (I can see you cringing. Yep. I am too.) It was so omnipresent in my life, it developed an antagonistic personality of its own: Itchy Demon.

I scratched it while I slept, so my mom clipped my nails short, put tube socks over my hands,

and pleaded with me to keep them on all night (I usually didn't).

I scratched it minutes after I slathered on a thick layer of yet another prescribed ointment or salve that didn't fulfill its promise to heal my broken skin. I remember the feeling of these creams building up under my fingernails while I dug down to scrape the redness, knowing with a heavy heart the relief I would feel would only lead to exponential misery later.

Sometimes I scratched just a little to see if that would be enough to appease it (it wasn't).

Sometimes I scratched it as hard as I could to see if my desperate, wild abandon might banish Itchy Demon once and for all (it didn't).

It was a miserable, endless, and cyclical experience. What was worse than the actual rash, though, was the fear that someone other than my family and my pediatrician would see it and either be completely horrified or tease me relentlessly about it in front of everybody, especially the cute boy(s) I had (a) crush(es) on.

When I had a particularly bad flare up, I felt I couldn't wear shorts like the other carefree kids who ran around the playground. I also obsessed for weeks over how I was going to survive yet another quarter of junior high swimming class where my secret might be found out by the pretty, popular girls by whom I so desperately wanted to be accepted. Here's the inner dialogue that happened every.damn.day:

"Okay, Carleen, stand over to the side with your back to the wall. They might see your calves, but that's not the worst part. Okay, get in the water quickly—that will help cover it up. Towel. Towel. Where's my towel? Oh, crap . . . Mrs. Witty is standing at the door of the group shower, checking off names. I am NOT going to get a decent grade in this class with my forlorn athletic ability, so I guess I have to make up some of those points by being humiliated . . . "

There was only one thing that stopped the creep of The Crud on my skin—escaping from the confines of my house and running through the woods with my dog in the springtime air. And there was only one thing that made the angry, red bumps go away, if only for just a few months—the water of Lake Vermilion. It kissed me and soothed me and told me that everything was going to be all right—that Dad was in his happy place on the boat and wouldn't yell at us, that wieners roasted over the fire were a delicacy, not a barely-getting-by meal, and that I could put my swimming suit on without fear because the girls who seemed to have it all together were off somewhere else being perfect.

Was it nature that ultimately healed me? I like to think that that's probably at least part of the answer. I can still feel the blissful feeling I had when I realized that Itchy Demon had been quieted. But I also knew from past experience that my reprieve would be temporary, and eventually the raging monster would wake up again as soon as the leaves began to change. And every year, the anticipation of my pain and helplessness grew worse and worse.

Thankfully, my skin issues cleared up sometime in high school. I'm not sure if I grew out of it or whether the family trauma I experienced around the age of fifteen made Itchy Demon stop and say, "Yeah—even I don't want to make this kid's life any worse." I do think it was a physical manifestation of Fear flooding my body, and scratching it was just a repeated, futile attempt to exorcise it.

To this day, I don't know if the kids at school noticed my Creeping Crud because no one ever said anything. I'm sure they were all busy worrying about their own perceived shortcomings. All I know for sure is that Alfred Hitchcock knew what he was talking about when he said, "There is no terror in the bang, only in the anticipation of it."

Just call me The Anticipator.

The Red Swimming Suit

When you were in swimming class at Virginia High School in the 1980s, you did not wear your own swimming suit like kids do today, and you certainly didn't have the option to wear a t-shirt over your suit. No . . . at that time, everyone had to wear a SCHOOL-ISSUED SWIMSUIT.

There are some definite benefits to this situation, of course. Like a school uniform, everyone looked the same—but let's just say these suits generally did not bring out our best features. There was no padding on top (read: glass cutters), the straps were all stretched out (necessitating having to be tied into the suit with a strip of material so it wouldn't fall down), and the suits were completely shapeless, so the girls who had something to show were just as covered up as those of us who had little to show (except the damn things didn't go down far enough to cover my Crud). Also, because school employees washed the suits every day in a hot, dingy-dark laundry room that looked like the first ring of hell, the only thing that sat in your locker and got moldy over the weekend was the towel you forgot to take home.

The biggest problem with those suits is that they were color-coded by size. I'm not kidding. Here's how that played out (picture an Awkward Adolescent Girl Bell Curve):

If you were one of the tiny girls (you know, the ones who still looked like they were in grade school, but you couldn't really hold it against them because they were in a cute category of their own), you wore a forest-green swimsuit. No big deal. There were just a couple of girls that size, and you kinda felt sorry for them because they didn't have any curves yet, and everyone knew from reading *Are You There God? It's Me, Margaret* that as adolescent girls, we were supposed to want boobs.

If you were an average-sized girl, you wore a red swimsuit. There were lots of red swimsuits on the pool deck because a lot of us were pretty average.

If you were even slightly above average, however, you were given a BLACK swimsuit. Yes, black is slimming, and I suppose we should have been grateful that that size wasn't white or beige, but when most of the people around you were wearing red, I'm guessing it didn't feel good at ALL. I don't remember ever thinking anything judgmental about anyone who wore black, but I do remember praying every year that I WOULD STILL FIT IN THE RED SUIT.

Now, we can write this off as a prac-

Swimsuits

Carleen: My swimsuits come in several categories:

- Unflattering/used to fit three years ago but who cares anyway
- Cute because board shorts.
- Comfortable as hell and puts AAAAALLLL my glorious cellulite out on Front Street.

I have had to talk myself through swimsuit experiences since I was thirteen years old. Once I get up to the cabin, I'm totally fine, especially with my body-positive nieces. In the "real world," though, I am admittedly PTSD about it. I need to desensitize and change my thinking. I need to bring my lake attitude home! The phrase "Put your damn swimsuit on" takes work.

Lisa: My current favorite swimming suit is one that I bought when I was pumped full of fertility drugs. I was in Breckenridge, Colorado, and I needed a suit. It's cute as hell but really expensive, because Breckenridge. It's only a little bit droopy in the ass—not bad though. I have been okay for the past several years regarding swimsuits, but there always is a little bit of terror because you truly are putting yourself out there when you put one on.

Carleen: My problem is that everything I am insecure about is cured by board shorts. Go into any store—99% of what they sell goes primarily above the belt. So, I have generally had a few choices:

1. Not swim
2. PTSD
3. Skirts
4. Internet shopping (#BoardShorts)
5. Not care

I am currently between 3 and 4. Gunning for #5.

These are my cousins and me at my cousin Peter's cabin (I think they are once removed or . . . something). They were always so stylish, and I was all, "Here's my hand-me-down suit—HIIII!" (#Lini)

ticality that helped the overworked ladies in the laundry room do their jobs so they could get out of their cave and back into polite society sooner than later. As we junior high girls filed by, stripped off our suits, and threw them on the pile, the color coding made it much faster the ladies to sort them, wash them, and put them back on the shelf for the next day's torture. (Did I mention I had Creeping Crud? And I had to strip off my suit at the laundry window and then walk in a line to the locker room to get my shampoo and towel? And that the only way I survived this without losing my sanity was by convincing myself that NO ONE REALLY NOTICED? Yeah. Just . . . yeah.)

We could also write off the whole situation as a nostalgic nod to a time when people just didn't pay as much attention to body size as we do now, or if they did, most people ascribed to the attitude of "Sucks to be you; you should have not had that sixth cupcake, then." Harsh? Sure, but back then, no one actually took the time to ask WHY someone ate that sixth cup-cake.

What we can't write off is the trauma that occurred when the Powers That Be decided that our swimming classes were going to be CO-ED. Yep, that's right. Starting in ninth grade, we had to swim with the boys. We had to sit up in the stands when we had our periods because we refused to wear tampons . . . with boys there. I had to try to cover up my Creeping Crud . . . with boys there. We had to try not to get hit in the face with faster-flying water polo balls . . . with boys there. And we had to wear shapeless, stretched-out, glass cutter-displaying, color-coded-by-size swimsuits . . . with boys there.

And those boys ALL wore black swimsuits. Every single one of them. It didn't matter how big or how small the boy was. His suit was BLACK. In their defense, I know they were probably self-conscious too, especially since these were Speedo-style swimsuits, not trunks, and there were no straps to secure them if they were saggy and in danger of falling down. But not ONE of those boys had to wonder what we were thinking about him because of the color of his suit. Not one of them had to pray that he would still fit in a red suit. Not one.

Sticky Note: The Writing Rah-Rah Speech

Some of you might be the kind of people who LURVE to write. Maybe you've kept a journal your whole life, maybe you've keep the world entertained with your social media posts, or maybe you've written a book yourself. Or maybe you haven't had time to do this because of

#AllTheThings, but you know deep down in your heart that if you had the time, something lovely to drink, and your special markers, you would be all over an opportunity to write because you know it's the stuff of fireworks and llamas doing the Electric Slide. If this is you, let's GO!

Some of you might be the kind who have written every now and then . . . maybe for work, maybe for a class, or maybe just for your shopping trip to Hy-Vee (or Kroger's/Cash Wise/Piggly Wiggly/Red Owl/Cub/Whole Foods/Whatever Your Food Emporium is). Writing to you is . . . fine? It gets the job done, but you just haven't had Atomic Starbursts go off very often, at least not to the level of #ElectricSlideLlamas. Hey, that's okay! Do what you need to do—let your words work for you as they always have. But stay open to the fireworks in case they decide to ignite this time. You never know! It could happen! If this is you, let's GO!

Some of you might hear words like "writing" and "journal questions" and "special markers" and break out in a cold sweat, ready to run for the hills of Bolivia. Maybe you've had people tell you in the past that you aren't a good writer (or worse yet, someone has made fun of or completely hacked apart something you wrote). Maybe you play the comparison game and say, "I just can't do what X can do, so I don't want to try. I'm going to sound stupid or completely inadequate." Maybe you write five pages and delete it because you think it's garbage. Maybe you just struggle and struggle to find just the right way to say things, and this experience tends to frustrate you more than having to walk away from a perfectly good mega-jar of #FakeFoodCheeseBalls (oh, why does the food industry mock us so?).

We want you to know that wherever you are, you have a voice that is beautiful because it is YOURS. You have a story. You have feelings. You have worth. You have something important to say. And what you write has the power to change the world, even if the only person who ever reads it is you. What affects one of us, affects all of us.

You can change your outlook, your understanding, and even your future as a result of listening to what your soul has to say, so be kind to your Little Writing Self. Let her speak without judging or correcting her. Let her describe what she senses and what she feels. Let her tell you what she

The Little TV

Love has been broadcast from the beginning of time. The #LoveWaves are all around you—all you have to do is tune in! If you don't like the channel, get up off the divan and change it!

Rule #1

thinks it all means. She is wise beyond her years—trust us. Trust her. The power of YOU preserving your stories in writing is absolutely IMMEASURABLE. So, if this is you, give writing a chance, and know that YOU are calling the shots, not the boat. Let's GO!

Chapter Four

YOUR TURN!
(JOURNAL QUESTIONS)

Take some time to write about Panic in your life. You might want to use some of the prompts below or go your own direction. Do what feels natural and right for you and listen to what your writing tells you about yourself and your life.

- Think about the kinds of situations in your life that typically cause you to "panic." What patterns do you see?

- What sources of "panic" come from inside of you?

- What sources of "panic" come from outside of you?

- Tell about a specific time when you felt "panic." What contributed to these feelings?

- Tell about a time when you should have felt "panic"—but you didn't! What made the difference?

- Has "panic" felt different at various times in your life? For example, is there a difference in how it hits you now vs. when you were young?

- Who are the people who stand with you and help you? What do they do for you?

- When have you positively helped others? Or, when could you positively help others in the future? What was that like/what could that be like for you?

- My biggest "a-ha" moment related to this section is . . . because . . .

- I hope to . . .

- I am grateful for . . .

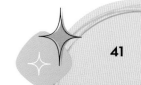

Rule #1

Chapter Five

#SPINGOLD: QUIET THE PANIC

Our Big Ol' Disclaimer: It is WELL established by now that we are NOT doctors, therapists, researchers, psychologists, or anything other than just regular, ordinary people. We have enough trouble figuring out social media, much less brains, psyches, and bodies. We have absolutely NO delusions of grandeur going on here!

So, please take our disclaimer into consideration when we offer up suggestions of things you can try to make your life more #EXTRA. We are well aware that we are not equipped or licensed to do anything other than just encourage you to try a few strategies if they feel right for you. We are just your Soul Sisters sitting around the table with you, shooting the sh*t while eating appetizers. We also pride ourselves in getting people to simultaneously laugh/cringe. So, if you do that along with us, we will be mighty pleased! And, OMG, if we can get you to snort? BONUS!

Also, we know from extensive personal experience that sometimes a girlfriend needs help from the Trained Professionals to get over the speed bumps of life, some of which have been around for much too long and have a nasty habit of flattening tires.

Here's the deal with that: WE LOVE US SOME THERAPY! It is totally #EXTRA to sit down with someone neutral, lay your "stuff" out on a hypothetical midcentury melamine table, and decide which things to toss, which things to return to others because they don't belong to you, which things to clean up a little, and which things to keep. It's like having someone help you clean out your purse. (Lots of us put that off until we just can't DEAL with it anymore, right? Wouldn't it be nice to have help with that task once in a while?) And, hey . . . sometimes you just need someone with the magic touch to help you adjust the dial of your perception just a titch so the image you're trying to see comes into focus a little better.

Okay, we're hearing some "buts" out there that we want to address.

BUT what if you think it's a sign of weakness to see a therapist and that you should be able to handle your problems yourself? News flash: when you're hurt physically, you go to the doctor, so why not seek help when you're hurt emotionally too—especially when there might be something chemically amiss in your brain? Just because it's not a visible broken arm or a more "acceptable" disease like cancer doesn't mean it's an illegitimate hurt.

If anyone says anything sideways about you being weak for caring for yourself, just say, "Bless your everlovin' heart," turn on your heel, and walk away. They would never say such a thing to you if you had cancer, so it shouldn't be acceptable for them to say something snarky to you about other kinds of hurts you're dealing with. (And they just might be projecting their own fears and doubts on to you because THEY have something going on that they don't want to deal with yet. That's not YOUR problem to solve #BecauseBoundaries. You do you. Let them do them.)

We could also argue that life is infinitely more stressful these days because it just KEEPS GO-ING 24/7 with no regard for rest. Because of this, we think it's good to bring in the #EXTRA reinforcements to counteract what we force our brains to deal with on too little sleep and too much caffeine. Right? Right!

BUT what if you are a religious person and think God should be able to solve all your prob-lems, so you should lean on God and not see a therapist? Look, we TOTALLY respect the wide variety of religious beliefs out there. We truly do! However, we want to offer this per-spective, which you are free to keep or toss: God truly does a happy dance when we help ourselves . . . plus, God gifted some people with the smarts and talent to become therapists. And—there are a lot of faith-based therapists out there who might make you feel more com-fortable.

We personally think God would be absolutely delighted to know you were taking advantage of the options out there that God actually set in motion, in the same way you appreciate someone who has the gift for making good red velvet cupcakes with cream cheese frosting. Or art. Or boat motors. Or whatever brings you joy. It's all good! Right? Right!

Okay, **BUT** what about the fear of other people finding out you need help? We each know this quite well.

Carleen: I wouldn't have been caught DEAD walking into the Range Mental Health

Center to talk about my brother's death by suicide in 1987. I already felt like people thought I was a little odd, and Teenage Me just wanted to fit in and maybe someday be accepted by the Inner Circle. (I did get invited to a toga party once. Thank you, Stacey, for inviting me.) Basically, being seen walking into a MENTAL HEALTH CENTER felt like a death warrant for my reputation.

Uh, hello??? Can we all agree that after thirty years, several rounds of depression/anxiety, and numerous soul-searching essays, MAYBE I would have suffered a little less if I hadn't given Fear so much power? My poor mother . . . she asked me several times to go, but I was too afraid that someone might SEE me. Sigh. I'm making up for it now, Mama.

Lisa: I would have been okay going in 1998. No one would have made me feel "other"— like I was different in an unacceptable way. But I did not want to go. I only felt about 5% stigmatized (my own doing), but I felt that no one would really have experience with my particular issue, so why would I go? I still feel this way today. I have always had a problem dredging things up or giving things life that I want to stay dead. I want negativity in my life to generally just BE dead. I went through the thing once, and I don't want to go through it again. So on a couple of different levels, I saw no point. I mean, this one was a no-brainer in my mind because there was literally nothing anyone could do for me.

And now I do have anxiety and depression, so I have continued to go off and on meds for the past ten years. And, quite frankly, nearly every single person I know has dealt with less-than-ideal circumstances in their life that have necessitated meds and/or therapy. I am currently combatting my stuff with essential oils, but not everyone can do that. There is absolutely no harm in trying, because nature has some great remedies, but sometimes a person just needs a little more help. What I have experienced is that meds can be helpful and therapy is extremely valuable. I strongly advise trying it if you have even one inkling you might need it. Sometimes dealing with your crap is above your own paygrade.

We are living in 2018 and beyond. If you still cringe at the possibility of public exposure, technology can be your friend because there are now ONLINE counseling options where you can video-conference with, email, and even text a licensed therapist. What's not to love about that? No one has to see you walking into the local mental health center, and no one needs to know unless you tell them. Right? RIGHT!

Okay . . . so let's say you've gotten out of your own way and are cool with seeing a

counselor/therapist/guru, BUT maybe you feel a little unsure about the treatment options #BecauseChemicalsEtc. We are here to tell you that there are lots of other strategies to try, and not all of them involve chemicals. There is no one way that works for everyone, and sometimes you just have to get your game on and see what works. For example . . .

Some people need to clean up their diets or figure out if there are foods that are not playing well with their systems (or if there are foods that would be good boosts for their systems). Some people need to move more or move differently. Some people need to find ways to express themselves creatively. Some people need to turn their focus to helping others instead of lamenting their deficiencies. Some people need vitamins and supplements. Some people need people in their lives to work on their own sh*t already, damn it. Some people need to feel a stronger connection to others. Some people need to meditate. Some people need to unlearn destructive patterns from childhood. Some people need a career change. Some people need to break up with a friend or family member that is bringing down their energy. Some people need to learn how to sleep better.

SOME PEOPLE NEED ALL OF THE ABOVE, but not necessarily in that order. The bottom line is, do what you need to do, Sister—we got you! There is absolutely NO shame in taking care of yourself, and remember, you call the shots, not the boat! Right? RIGHT!

Now that we got all that off our chests, here are a few things to ponder, take, or leave, even if the most they amount to are suggestions to get you through a rough moment (or ten). Each section of the book will have a few for your consideration (because while this could be considered a self-help book, it's not really . . . it kind of defies categorization, which is EXACTLY the way we want it).

We don't want to TELL you how to help yourself . . . we just want to toss out some nudgy ideas because the point of this book is to encourage you not to get stuck in misery. Nope! The key is to acknowledge the issue, figure out where it came from, if possible, listen to what it can teach you, and then MOVE ON. It's much better to #SpinGold (grow from a rotten situation and/or focus on love) because that's what's going to make your life—and the world—better.

Just remember that there are no magic bullets in life. There just aren't. So, focus on doing the #NextRightThing for you, even if it's something really simple. No matter how small the step, the goal is to keep moving forward as much as possible.

Now that we've gotten THAT out of the way, let's consider some suggestions we have for dealing with Panic.

(Hey! We have the sneaking suspicion you have some awesome self-care strategies to share with the group that have already worked for you. Visit www.getupandtryagain.com, click on #SelfCareStrategies, and send them in!)

Idea #1: Soothe Your Inner Child

There is a great story by Sandra Cisneros called "Eleven" that every adult should read. The opening paragraphs go like this:

> What they don't understand about birthdays and what they never tell you is that when you're eleven, you're also ten, and nine, and eight, and seven, and six, and five, and four, and three, and two, and one. And when you wake up on your eleventh birthday you expect to feel eleven, but you don't. You open your eyes and everything's just like yesterday, only it's today. And you don't feel eleven at all. You feel like you're still ten. And you are—underneath the year that makes you eleven.
>
> Like some days you might say something stupid, and that's the part of you that's still ten. Or maybe some days you might need to sit on your mama's lap because you're scared, and that's the part of you that's five. And maybe one day when you're all grown up, maybe you will need to cry like if you're three, and that's okay. That's what I tell Mama when she's sad and needs to cry. Maybe she's feeling three.
>
> Because the way you grow old is kind of like an onion or like the rings inside a tree trunk or like my little wooden dolls that fit one inside the other, each year inside the next one. That's how being eleven years old is.

Isn't that writing gold? You are never simply "just" the age you are, chronologically. You are #AllTheAges! Adults should feel free to express childlike wonder, go on adventures, and giggle about something completely silly if they want to. It is okay to feel fear, to need comfort, and to stomp around just a little bit when you're frustrated (as long as you don't hurt others). It's okay to make mistakes. It's okay to be proud of yourself. It's okay to need time with a friend, even when there are bills to pay and floors to mop more than three times a year.

Something happens to us along the way when we forget we are #AllTheAges. Maybe it starts in the teen years, when we can't WAIT to grow up, get our driver's license, and get a job . . . things that make us feel like an adult with limitless power and freedom. Maybe someone tells

us we need to buck up, stop whining, and grow up already. Or maybe we are praised when we keep our cool and shamed when we don't.

Reality check—Little You is still inside you and will always be part of you, no matter how big, stinky, and important you get, and sometimes she needs to be comforted.

Why is this so hard? We know it's important to have connections with others . . . friends, family members, and even random people you meet in line at the smoothie place. They support you, build you up, and even help you hide a dead body when required (but we don't recommend that) (too much? ;). Equally important, though, is being connected to yourself. And sometimes your inner child needs you to be her big sister.

Me and my mama in Anchorage, Alaska, where I was born. I used to tell people that I was an Eskimo . . . mainly because I thought I was one. (#Lili)

I (Carleen) worked with a great counselor once who had a wonderful technique for self-soothing that she shared with me during what I call the Twilight Zone of my life (read: majorly traumatic experience that hung on and on and on). She asked, "What is a small, special object to you that would bring you comfort—maybe something that will remind you of being a littler version of yourself? When you find that thing, I'd like you to carry it with you. And when you feel the panic starting to rise, touch it and say to Little You, "I won't let anything hurt you."

It took a while, but I eventually figured out the perfect thing—I made a friendship pin, like we used to do in the early '80s. I clipped it on my work ID lanyard, and no one noticed it. It was my private, subtle communication device with my inner child. It worked like a charm.

Eat? Is it cake? Why, yes! (#Lini)

(If you don't know what a friendship pin is, here's the backstory: Around 1982 or so, we kiddies started making friendship pins to trade with one another and wear in bunches on the top part of our tennis shoe laces. You'd go to Ben Franklin or wherever and buy a bunch of beads of different shapes and colors, and you'd string them on the pointy part of a safety pin and give them to your friends.)

Our version of the iconic friendship pin: four colors to represent the Four Rules of Life, According to Waterskiing, plus a heart to remind you that you matter, just as you are. #LeadWithLove

It just so happened this therapist-suggested Inner Child Support Object strategy coincided with a recent social movement where people wore safety pins to show that they were supportive of immigrant families in our country. For me, wearing a friendship pin at that particular time took on an extra meaning—it was a way to tell my students and their parents that I loved and supported them. I ended up making a bunch for my office mates, which also made me feel good. It was an important #SpinGold moment.

If you try this technique, pick something that works for you . . . maybe it's a smooth stone, a coin, a piece of ribbon, or something #EXTRA special from your childhood. Ascribe meaning to it to give your Little Self the love and comfort she needs to not feel alone.

(Now, we know that some of you realists are saying, "Really . . . ?" We get it . . . because we live with realists. If this sounds corny to you, then skip it! But it just might surprise you, and no one has to know you're doing it if you keep it to yourself, right? Right!

Idea #2: Breathe. Just . . . Breathe.

One of the darlingest things in the world—but you can't ever SAY ANYTHING ABOUT THIS OUT LOUD TO ANYONE, OR THEY MAY MELT FROM EMBARRASSMENT—are hyper-nervous teenagers. They come in several varieties.

Some of them feel a special kind of pressure to be tough, strong, and silent, no matter what, and they generally pull it off . . . unless they have to perform in some way. Others are more comfortable expressing their fears out loud—usually in the form of blurting, talking, complaining, whining, or straight out telling you they-are-so-nervous-they-just-might-die.

Some of them get louder, punch each other, and knock things over accidentally. Others slink down behind a book or under the table, hoping you won't notice them. Some of them look to see what the most popular kid is doing and do that. All of them have an issue with breathing.

Does any of this sound familiar? Wait, what? It's not just your kiddos having this issue? ;)

Breathing, it turns out, is exactly what all of us need to do more. According to all yoga teach-

ers and most therapists, knowing how to breathe is absolutely an essential way to help us calm our minds and our bodies. Someone telling you to breathe probably feels like a please-tell-me-you're-not-serious no-brainer. However, the majority of us have somehow forgotten the benefits of breathing deeply from our bellies, something Little We did quite naturally before #AllTheThings. Instead, we deprive ourselves of Oxygen Goodness by breathing shallowly and/or hyperventilating.

In yoga, breath is called pranayama, or the life force breath. I (Lisa) have been doing yoga for almost fifteen years, and every single yoga teacher I have ever had has addressed our breath and how to access it. There are powerful body and mind benefits to knowing your breath and how to control it. When I start to panic, my breathing becomes shallow and quick. I feel like I am breathing from the bottom of my throat, and air isn't even entering my lungs. I have also been to a lot of therapy (on my own and with others), and I have learned that when you breathe deeply, it sends a message to your brain to slow your heart rate. This combats the cortisol that is released when you are panicking and helps you feel calmer.

I (Carleen) use a technique called Square Breathing to deal with nerves and anxiety. It goes like this:

1. Take a slow, deep breath in through your nose for a count of four (make it slow and steady).
2. Hold your breath for a count of four.
3. Exhale through your mouth for a count of four, getting as much air out of your lungs as possible.
4. Hold your breath at the bottom for another count of four.
5. Repeat two to three times until you feel calmer.

Any quality meditation leader will encourage you to focus on your breath and leave the stressful somethings behind for a while. They aren't going anywhere, and they might look different once your body is calmer.

Idea #3: Power Posing

Another variation on the theme of using mindfulness to deal with Panic is called Power Posing. Now, there has been some back-and-forth on whether this is "real" #BecauseScience or not. If you haven't heard about this episode of Social Psychology Smack Down, here's the Reader's Digest Condensed Version, followed by our reasoning for using it. (We should note that 2018 #BecauseScience is in favor of it.)

Power Posing gained popularity in 2012 when Harvard researcher Amy Cuddy did a TED Talk about the practice of standing in a position of power for a couple of minutes to prepare for a stressful or challenging experience. (Picture Wonder Woman or Superman with their hands planted firmly on their hips, their chests out, and their heads up in a "What's up?" position.)

Power Posing is all about choosing body language that makes you feel powerful, strong, and worthy of taking up space (something we women are not always encouraged to do). It makes sense, doesn't it? How we hold our bodies affects how we think and feel about them and ourselves—it's why our mothers told us to sit up straight and put a smile on our faces.

Cuddy stated that not only did people feel better from Power Posing—it also had a positive effect on a person's hormones by increasing testosterone and decreasing cortisol, the stress hormone that we all need MUCH less of. People started doing it before sporting events and job interviews (and we wouldn't be surprised if there was some Power Posing being done in coffee shop bathrooms before a few first dates too).

There arose a bit of a hubbub, however. Some of Cuddy's colleagues challenged the validity of her research, and for a while, people considered Power Posing to be pseudoscience. However, in 2018, Cuddy published another study that provided scientific validity about the first claim, at least—that people who practiced Power Posing did, in fact, feel more powerful. There was no good replication of the hormone claim of the first study.

What is interesting to us (in the context of this book) are some assertions made by Kim Elsesser, a contributor to *Forbes* magazine, who wrote about Cuddy's work. One of Elsesser's theories is that Cuddy was criticized because she is a successful woman who wanted to empower other women (hmmmm!!). Elsesser also states that researchers sometimes label studies that are interesting and understandable by the public as being flawed.[1]

Now, we aren't brainiacs . . . we spill coffee on our white shirts as we read social media posts,

just like everyone else. We just don't get ourselves tangled up in the minute complexities of #BecauseScience because . . . #AllTheThings. (Maybe you do, and that's great!) Instead, we like us some relatable practical knowledge, and we love us some female empowerment.

Here's what we do know: Power Posing works for us! Aligning yourself with strong women in your mind can make you feel DAMN POWERFUL, so WHY NOT strike a pose? You aren't hurting anyone if you do it, right? Of course not! And let's be honest . . . who doesn't love a little Wonder Woman or Notorious RBG in her life? We may be grown-ups, but it's totally okay to let our Little Selves choose a powerful alter ego now and then. We did it with Underoos back in the day, so we can totally do it again.

So, go ahead, Sisters . . . put your hands on your hips and rock your #EXTRASheroSelf if you feel like it . . . and send a picture or two to us on www.getupandtryagain.com if you are so moved!

Idea #4: Thirty-Second Dance Party, à la Grey's Anatomy

Lots of people watch the TV show *Grey's Anatomy* for the eye candy, whether you are current with the show's timeline or are just discovering it on Netflix, like Carleen's teenager. Even if you don't know a single thing about the plot (or care, for that matter), we are confident you will agree that Shonda Rhimes assembled a good-looking cast with someone for everyone (*cough cough* McDreamy). (Um, hello, Carleen . . . McSteamy was MUCH hotter. Everyone knows that. —Lisa)

Another beautiful thing to come out of that show is the idea that a Thirty-Second Dance Party, even if it's a party of one, can be an #EXTRA good stress reliever and panic dissolver. There's a great scene where Meredith walks in to a room to find Cristina dancing away, throwing her awesome hair back and forth. Meredith starts babbling on about her woes, and Cristina yells, "Shut up! Dance it out!" Meredith dances—and talks a little more about what she's going to do. Cristina says, "Whatever!" and keeps dancing. At the end of the segment, she yells, "Dancing makes you BRAVE!"

We think this is an #EXTRA awesome idea! (There is a lot of #BecauseScience behind it that we could get into, like how dancing stimulates endorphins, oxytocin, etc., but we're guessing that's not a super-duper new idea to anyone. See more about the benefits of moving your body in chapter 20.)

Me and my dad at Plymouth, Mass. in 1976. I loved that outfit! (#Lili)

Those pants. And—one of my heroes, my Big Brother Kevin. Cat and dog eyes in the background. (#Lini)

It doesn't matter if you are a good dancer or not—just crank up a song you love (like "Africa" by Toto or Weezer or WHAT-EVS), turn down your brain, and boogie down for a little while—for thirty seconds or for the whole damn song. We guarantee you will feel better, and you may just shake loose a little bit of something that is holding you back. (Don't think about the jiggly bits. Just dance!)

You can even do it in your car. There are definitely people out there in the Twin Cities metro who could attest they've seen us singing at the top of our lungs and dancing behind the steering wheel (most likely to "Let's Go Crazy" by Prince, our hometown guy, or something from *Hamilton*). As long as you stay in your lane and obey traffic laws, who cares if you aren't scowling and staring forward like everyone else on the road? Be #EXTRA! Dance it out! You might even inspire someone else to smile or even wiggle their butt a little bit. BAM! You just made a positive difference in the world.

You can even do it in the bathroom—shut the door if it makes you feel better. No one needs to see if you don't want an audience. It can just be the music, your shimmying buttski, and you.

Wherever you do it, take it easy and be careful not to pull a muscle. Not kidding.

Idea #5: Oils We Like for This

Ginger
Cinnamon Bark
Lavender
Lemon
Peppermint
Cedarwood
Vetiver
Orange
Sandalwood

Why We Love Oils

#BecauseTheyWorkForUs
#SpeakingOnBehalfOfJustUs
#NotDoctorsJustPeople
#JustSayin
#SkepticalHusbandsRecant
#ThatIsHuge
#SrslyUHaveNoIdea
#Versatile
#Noses
#Throats
#Tummies
#Mood
#Cramps
#HotFlashQuickFix
#Relaaaaax
#ForTheLoveOfAllThatIsHolyGetRidOfThatSmell
#AchesAndPains
#AllTheThings
#SorryForTheRantIWasntProperlyOiled
#ActualTextFromMichelleToLisa@Sisters
#PeppermintBrownies
#LavenderFieldsForever
#TheresAnOilForThat
#100%Natural
#NoThankYouChemicals
#HopOffMyEndocrineSystem
#BuhBye

Lavender Fields Forever (#Lili)

Rule #2

IF YOU FALL,
FALL GRACEFULLY

Chapter Six

DUUUDE, THAT'S A GNARLY SCAR

Dear Lovelies,

Falling down is something that comes easily to all of us—too damn easily.

It starts off innocently enough, doesn't it? When we're babies, we figure out how our bodies work, eager to get moving under our own power so we can go after what we want on the other side of the room. Everyone from our parents to our aunties are eager to help us take our first steps—they hold onto our hands and encourage us with squeals of excitement, telling us that we can do it, we can do it, WE CAN DO IT! Oh, what big Little Humans we are!

Do we do it perfectly the first time? The second time? The fifth time? Of course not! We're Wobbly Crazy-Feet Humans. We're cute, little mobile disasters. We trip over things, we knock things over by mistake, and we smack our heads on the concrete or the sharp edge of the coffee table.

All that is par for the course, and no one around us thinks twice about it. All they focus on is where we're headed, what we'll eventually be able to do, and what they need to do to make our environment safer for us until we get the hang of mobility. All we focus on is getting to the next place we want to be or the next thing we want to get our hands on.

The falling continues as we move into childhood. Riding a bike, skateboarding, climbing trees, swinging in the park, ice skating, snowboarding . . . name the activity—there's bound to be falling. Again, we don't care! We just want to do and be and discover and conquer our little corner of the world. And the encouraging continues, if we have good support in our lives. Try again, kiddo. You'll get it next time. Try it this way. Make this little adjustment. You can do it.

59

We know you can.

We also try new things when it comes to our emotions and our interpersonal relationships. We ask the kid with the curly hair playing in the sandbox if we can play too. We stay overnight at a new friend's house, even though we're nervous about being away from home. We stand up to the bully on the playground who's hurting our friend.

It would be great if every situation worked out perfectly on the first try, but that doesn't always happen. Sometimes the curly-haired kid starts to ignore you because you don't want to get your white knee socks dirty. Sometimes you lie awake at night under your friend's canopy bed, missing your mom. Sometimes the bully steals your new Snoopy hat off your head and demands you bring her packs of Hubba Bubba if you ever want to see it again.

Emotional and interpersonal dilemmas like those aren't super hard to solve when you're a kid. You find a new friend to play with on the monkey bars. You dig down deep and find the strength to close your eyes, knowing you'll get to go home again in the morning. You ask your mom to help you deal with the bully, and she tells you to tell her to give it back, or else your mom will make her give it back.

As we grow, however, the physical, emotional, and interpersonal dilemmas we encounter get more complex, and the stakes become higher. We ask ourselves things like:

- Should I date this person?
- Should I use chemicals?
- What college should I go to?
- What job is right for me?
- Should I marry this person?
- Where should we live?
- Do we get a dog?
- Do we want two or four kids?

And some of us must ask different, more difficult questions that don't necessarily have easy answers, like, how do I even begin to deal with the effects of:

- Growing up with abuse?
- Being in an abusive relationship?
- Struggling with a serious physical or mental health issue of mine (or someone else's)?
- Finding my way through financial struggles?

- Dealing with significant loss(es)?
- Being mistreated or bullied because of my race, gender, socioeconomic status, belief system, or orientation?

Maybe you see yourself or people that you know and love all over those questions. Maybe you have questions to add. Whatever your situation, we hear you, we see you, and we love you. Always. We know that issues like this—issues that you did not choose for yourself—add layers of pain to the already challenging task of being human. We want to acknowledge this and encourage you to speak out and share your truth about how this has affected you in hopes that you will find healing and love on the other side of struggle.

Sometimes we celebrate, and sometimes we commiserate. Either way, we call these events #WhiskeyDiscussions (complete with our Hamilton shot glasses, when we remember them).

No matter how old you get, you will continually have to figure out who you are, where you're going, what you want, who you can trust, and how this crazy mass of bones and skin works (because it didn't come with an owner's manual, damn it).

And guess what? Even though we're grown, we still fall down. Humans just DO, for better or for worse. Sometimes we fall accidentally, sometimes we get lazy, sometimes we make bad decisions, and sometimes we remain tangled up in the quagmire of our childhood pain, we make HUGE mistakes. Big ones. BIG.

The conundrum is that when you're a grown-up, other grown-ups assume you have it ALL figured out, so if you fall, you suck. It's your fault, you should have known better, you're weak, you're selfish, you're stupid, and so on. We become overwhelmed by this Chorus of Judgement that permeates everything, including our relationship with ourselves.

To complicate matters, we don't always have a team of supportive people around us as adults like we did when we were kids. We might not have anyone helping us up, cheering us on, or telling us that we can do it because they know we can. Nope. Sometimes it's just the opposite—some people unapologetically love a good train wreck and use it as a way to make themselves feel superior (despite being equally human).

As a result, something incredibly sad happens: Fear finds us, and all of a sudden, we find ourselves on lonely teams of TWO. Us and Fear. Fear and us. Whether it's brought on by experiences we can't control, sh*tty people in our lives, some sort of injury, or too much trauma all at once, Fear sets up camp in our souls and commences ripping us apart, piece by piece by piece.

Yeah . . . we all definitely fall down as grown-ups. Sometimes, it's a Wipeout for the Ages.

So how DO we fall gracefully, à la Rules of Life as Illustrated by Waterskiing? What in the world does that even LOOK like? That's what we're going to explore in this section.

BFF,

Lisa and Carleen

P.S. We didn't really talk about the title of this section, did we? Duuude . . . that's a gnarly scar. Do you hear a surfer dude? Duuude. Duuuuuude. Some people just love wipeout stories, especially if you lived to tell about it AND have a gnarly scar to prove that you went through something freakish. It's a badge of honor. Physical scars are more lauded and magnified than emotional scars, though. No one says, "Duuuuuuuude . . . that's a gnarly emotional scar you've got there. Look at that thing. That must have been some wipeout, maaaaaannnnn."

Chapter Seven

LISA STORIES

Slam Dunk

I fell in love with the love of my life in an education class at Minot State University in 1990. With the help of a pastel, V-neck, yellow shaker sweater that I wore backwards (on purpose), my most excellent flower pants, and a sassy attitude, he fell in love with me right back. It was a slam dunk! He was more of a straight arrow than I was, as my true badassery started to come in when I was a senior in high school/freshman in college. By our sophomore year, my #BFF Amy and I both were seriously honing our badass skills. We had zero self-esteem issues, especially when we walked into a room together. Anyway, Paul, Love of My Life, was first a member of the College Democrats and later, when I met him, a member of the Young Republican group on campus. I was not conservative, AT ALL, but this difference just made us laugh! We would cancel each other's votes, just like my Grandma Bert and Grandpa Ing used to do.

Anyway, I decided I would get him interested in me by calling him at Video Magic, where he worked. I knew he was working that night because Video Magic was just a few blocks from my house, and his tan Suzuki Samurai was sitting in the lot. #NotAStalker. So, my great idea was I would call and tell him that I heard he could recommend some good porn. Yep. I did that! I thought I was so clever, and apparently he didn't think I was too crazy because that stunt didn't end any potential relationship right there on the spot!

Paul was smart, handsome, witty, fun, and the president of the student body. He was the total package, and I was head over heels in lurve. He related with everyone and could talk to anyone. You really would be hard-pressed and kind of a dick not to like him. And if he liked you, he tended to tease and pick on you mercilessly. Sorry, Amy and Gina! I was not exempt, but he tended to lay off me per my multiple threats to his longevity!

He had (still has) a wonderful family. I loved (still love) them all. And he was mine. Minus one breakup, it was a done deal. He was a year ahead of me, and he landed his first teaching and coaching job in Mohall, North Dakota. He lived forty-five minutes away while I finished my final year of college. We were broke as hell, but solidly on the happily-ever-after track. Solid-ly. A surer thing certainly did not exist. Anywhere. We got married immediately after I graduated from college. Done deal. Slam dunk. And if you know Paul at all, you will appreciate the nod to basketball.

After not such a great year teaching in Wisconsin, my first year and his second, we both landed teaching jobs in Northfield, Minnesota. We had great jobs, great friends, great students, and a great life! We moved apartments a few times and finally were able to build a townhome in Burnsville (the big city, you know!). And it was supposed to last forever, except it didn't.

I went through a scrapbook phase in my early twenties. Can you tell? Res isn't great, but just like life, you get what you get! This is Paul and me at our first job fair in Missoula, MT. (#Lili)

We didn't get our happily ever after. He had circumstances he became aware of when we'd been together for eight years. Well, he always kind of knew, but was desperately trying not to acknowledge it. It became abundantly clear to him once he left teaching and started working in the financial sector in downtown Minneapolis. If anyone was capable of willing something away, it would have been him, but he couldn't . . . because life doesn't work that way. And you can't pray the gay away. Some people can avoid it forever, but I can't imagine a more miserable existence. No one deserves that. Everyone deserves to be happy.

Anyway, we couldn't be together anymore, and I thought I was dying. I did not think it was possible to be more heartbroken than me . . . but he actually was. He was completely shattered. He had exploded into a million little shards of glass, and I had a snap decision to make. Do I support him or turn against him? But really, there was no decision to be made, was there? Well, WAS there? The answer, people, is NO. This person was my partner, my best friend, my love, my husband, the person I was going to grow old with. Yes, I was losing him, but I figured if I ever loved him at all, I needed to stick by him and see him through. How was I going to abandon him in his time of need? I didn't think twice. I felt terribly sad and broken, and very lost. Okay, I was completely destroyed. But our love was strong, our support system was strong, and we both made it through. Also, I would rather have had him here and not be with him than not have him here. Make sense?

He knew he had my support 100 percent, and that made all the difference. It was the nicest, most pleasant divorce ever. It really was. He took care of me in many, many ways before and after the divorce. I also had his 100 percent support. After we signed the final papers at the courthouse, he took me out for dinner. He paid my undergrad loan off. He helped me find an apartment and paid the deposit and the first month's rent. He gave me all our possessions, except for the TV. All he wanted was that TV. And if you know Paul at all, you will laugh at the nod to his love for television programming.

He could not have been a better human being. He took care of things. He took care of me. He checked in on me about every six months to make sure I was okay, even when I went radio silent for a few years. The processing years.

Much has transpired since. He always wanted to be Uncle Paul to all my kiddos, and so he is. Today he is one of my best friends on the face of this earth. He always has been. He is a for-ever person. And so is Uncle Fabrizio, his husband and partner of twenty years. Wonderful, wonderful humans! So, even though it was not at ALL my plan (like, not even a little bit), it worked out in the end. I fell gracefully because I had to. We both depended on it. I had to be strong because there was no other choice. I let go of the rope. Major wipeout. Hanging onto my life jacket by one strap, I let him go.

These Boots Were Made for Walking

Pretty big boots to fill! (#Lili)

I have always been a stubborn and steadfast protector of my peace. I tend to shut panic down by swiftly controlling the situation. If I can shut the panic down and provide a comfort cushion, then I can more easily control the fall. I had no idea why I did this when I was younger . . . or older. I was no mastermind in that regard, I just knew what I needed to do to stay in balance, to provide cushion for any potential falls, to avoid a total crash and burn. To be perfectly honest, I didn't really figure this out until recently. I have just been doing it as a matter of course. A matter of survival.

In the seventh grade, I made a new friend. This friend was pretty, curled her hair, wore makeup, and was so cool! Her dad taught at Minot State University and she had two older sisters; hence, she knew what cool was, AND how to be it. Her sisters had all the cool posters, clothes, deodorants, and perfumes. It was an education just being in their rooms! They had Jelly Bellies AND HBO at her house! I had never heard of either. First, I didn't know that jelly beans could be anything other than the kind that I searched for on Easter morning, and, OMG, how cool was *Fraggle Rock*? I also loved that we could sometimes tune into naughty programs late at night! So, basically, she was on a different track than me. She eventually met a friend at school who was beautiful, exactly like her, AND a little naughty. That is when my friend started smoking. I was pretty bummed. I spent a month talking to her about it, but the draw of the naughty was too intoxicating for my friend, and that is what she chose. I could join her or walk away. I walked away. For three or four months, the two of them gave me a hard time for choosing to turn away, but they eventually got bored and left me alone. Sometimes you have to walk away from friendships that don't serve you to preserve your sense of balance in the world.

Okay . . . Fine. I'll Listen.

I've come to realize I'm a super-duper control freak when it comes to my happiness and comfort level, and I think it has served me relatively well. It helps with the graceful falling thing. And I have fallen on my face several times. It's not like I don't sit with my pain, I do. I sit with it and I work through it, because that is where the learning is. But I also have my carefully crafted butt donut. I don't wish to control anyone else, but I WILL control my environment to the best of my ability. Disclaimer: My inclusive nature means I am the queen of giving someone the benefit of the doubt and several chances. Having said that, if you get in the way of my happiness, you might get a llama kick and you might never hear from me again. When I exit, I try to exit gracefully. I don't want to hurt anyone or make a fuss. But I don't have the time or energy to deal with negative or problem-causing people. I just avoid them. And I'm quite good at it. I need my energy for more important things like my family, my friendships, getting enough sleep, staying healthy, and making a positive impact on people. So, I don't have time for that crap and I won't make time, either. Hard. Line. Drawn. Don't mess with my balance. I give fair warning: I will make corrections. Nothing personal, it's just what keeps me sane. It is also what keeps my kidneys healthy. In all seriousness, I have to be able to control those numbers and keep them low.

Okay, so, kidneys.

I was diagnosed with chronic kidney disease (CKD) in 2009. It's not something genetic or hereditary. It came from four years of sustained stress. The kind of stress that turns your stomach into knots. The kind of stress that gives you migraines when you have never had them before. The kind of stress that almost lands you in the hospital for physical issues, emotional issues, or both. I knew the saying "Stress Can Kill," but I guess I didn't really think I would walk away from a stressful situation with damaged kidneys. My body was telling me something. It was screaming at me, and I didn't listen to it for a long time. I was waiting for things to resolve themselves. But they didn't. And I am being vague on purpose. I am not ready to talk about this in detail. Things happened, and I reacted until there was nothing left to do except move forward.

It was shortly after that when my doctor noticed I had abnormally high blood pressure. Since I had always been very healthy, she ordered panels. That is when we discovered that my kidneys were damaged. The stress caused high blood pressure that caused my numbers to be consistent with chronic kidney disease. I have no physical symptoms except occasional fatigue. But let's be real. The fatigue could be caused by ten other things. The illness is manageable. Being able to manage the fatigue is debatable.

With a few lifestyle changes, I can mostly control the numbers. I hang out between stage 1 and 2. My most recent panels (one day before writing this), I was at a stage 1. My basic metabolic panel was fine (kidney function is fine), but my microalbumin level (albumin is blood protein) was elevated. That is the telltale sign of early CKD because kidneys are not supposed to leak microalbumin. Maybe this is TMI, but if you are reading this and you have long-term sustained stress in your life, please do something about it. I take meds to control the high blood pressure (because apparently that is not going away), but CKD is not curable. So, stop being so damn stressed out! You don't want a disease you can't get rid of because your stress levels were/are out of control and you didn't take the time or energy to manage it.

Chapter Eight

CARLEEN STORIES

Darkness and Light

When you're a kid, you live under the umbrella of your parents' control and influence—eating what they put in front of you, going to bed when they tell you to, watching and listening to what they deem appropriate, and following the rules they say exist for your own good. For the most part, you feel safe. Curious. Happy. Protected.

At some point, though, you find yourself ready to spread your teenage wings and leave the nest in pursuit of your own dreams. Homework, chores, and family drama are still a thing, so you cope by losing yourself on purpose with music, friend adventures, and an emotion you're pretty sure is love. You don't cherish the boundaries and rules your parents maintain, and you certainly can't admit you feel more secure knowing someone is still looking out for you and your well-being. You push the envelope, experiment, and explore who you are. You try on masks. You begin to grapple with the Big Questions. You start figuring yourself out.

That was definitely me when I was fifteen—that is, until the bottom fell out of my life. During the cold, dark winter of 1987, my brilliant Big Brother Cedric died by suicide.

Unless you've lost someone to suicide, it's impossible to get your head around how insidious it is and how it changes The Living forever. It's a roiling, stifling smog of guilt and grief that permeates every corner of your being. It is an angry, poisonous, despair-filled loneliness. It is, in a word, unimaginable.

And when you are the youngest child in a family affected by suicide, your entire concept of safety, stability, and protection disintegrates in one horrific instant. Suicide separates you from someone you love, but it also separates you from parts of yourself you spend the rest of your life trying to recover. Suicide snuffs out pure light and replaces it with a weak, green, flickering fluorescent bulb that threatens to burn out at any moment.

My mother wailed like a mortally wounded animal the afternoon she heard her firstborn son had taken his life. I can't begin to fathom her experience now that I am a mother. She spent every desperate, lonely day for two whole years crying after the rest of us left for work and school. She was completely overcome by her grief, but she kept it to herself because she didn't want to burden us. I don't know how we failed to notice, but I suppose it was because we too were grieving. We couldn't see past our own pain. We didn't know how desperately she had needed someone—anyone—to see her until years later.

My father also suffered silently, although he loudly went over and over the facts of what had happened, trying to make sense of the senselessness and find someone to blame. He opened up to a relative decades later, admitting through tears that he ultimately blamed himself for Cedric's death. It's not a secret that their relationship was strained at best. But what happened to Cedric was no one person's fault, and I have no doubt the burden of my dad's shame took a toll on every aspect of his health.

My sister and my other brother, both of whom were also extra parents to me, had to deal with their own deep grief at a time when their attention should have been focused on developing careers and raising children. Instead of hitching their wagons to stars as they set off to make their mark on the world with their creativity and optimism, they were forced to mark time. They had to reconcile Cedric's painful past with their own, haunted by what-ifs, if-onlys, and if-I-had-knowns.

And me? I got lost.

I used to walk through the sea of Cedric's boxes in our basement, wondering why he had left me. Didn't he love me? Wasn't I important to him? Wasn't I enough light to fight off the darkness inside him? There must have been something wrong with me, I reasoned—otherwise, he would have never, ever left me.

The last known picture of Big Brother Cedric—on a train in Alaska. We found it on some undeveloped film in his stuff after he died. (#Lini)

We all entertained impossible questions that had no answers. How could Cedric choose drowning in the January waters of the Mississippi River over living? How could he

have determined that the world was too painful to endure? How could he have ever believed that leaving us was the best option available to him? We didn't understand clinical depression then; all we understood was that our hearts ached and desperately wanted to find some meaning in the madness. And because we didn't have the closure of seeing him in an open casket, we sometimes had a hard time believing he was gone.

Our disbelief led us to consider the possibility that my computer- and math-loving brother was not really dead. Maybe he'd actually entered the Witness Protection Program because of the important work he had to do to save the world. For many years, I looked for him at every crowded mall and remote gas station, hoping a glimpse of his face would allow me to release the crushing pain and abandonment I felt.

Some of my friends, unfamiliar with processing grief, told me after a few months, "You're using your brother's death as an excuse to be mad at us." This feels terribly insensitive, but had the tables been turned, I wouldn't have known how to comfort such paralyzing grief, either.

There came a point when I couldn't take the darkness inside of me anymore, and I needed to rid myself of it. I'm not sure when I threw on the light switch, but at some point that year, I transformed myself into the epitome of 1980s sunshine and happiness. I laughed a LOT, I wore bright clothing, I listened endlessly to bubble-gum pop music, and I shied away from anything that remotely reminded me of pain, conflict, or isolation. I surrounded myself with

It Was All About the Music . . . And the Mixtapes!

Lisa: I was definitely catching the rays down in Africa. It was all about catching the rays in the '80s. What did you hear??

Carleen: Yeah. So I sang, "I miss the rains down in Africa," about a million gazillion times. What was that, nostalgia? The Anxiety Monster? My bleeding heart?

Toto AND Weezer: It's "I bless the rains, you guys . . ." *facepalm*

I sat for endless hours creating the perfect playlist on this stereo. Fingers on play and record, hoping that the DJ didn't talk when the song began OR ended. And then rewind, rewind, rewind so that I could write down the lyrics! (#Lili)

palm trees and pink flamingos and turquoise-colored bedroom walls, and I immersed myself in my friends' happy families instead of my own broken one.

My mother looked at me one day and said, "Why are you so HAPPY? It's not NORMAL." I brushed off her concern, along with her attempt to get me to see a counselor. I told her I was absolutely and completely fine, and besides, I would have been MORTIFIED to walk through the doors of a mental health clinic (something you just didn't do in a small northern Minnesota town in the '80s).

I didn't stop long enough to hear what she really meant: "What you're showing the world is the complete opposite of what I feel, and I am utterly miserable."

What my mom didn't hear in my self-assured response was that I was feeling exactly the same way. The difference was that I needed to be just GREAT! in everyone's eyes so I had a chance of surviving not only my teenage years, but also one of the most tragic events a kid can experience.

Looking back, I feel guilty I didn't spend more time with my family, battling the grief with them instead of leaving them to wrestle it alone. But I just couldn't do it. I couldn't feel that crushing pain anymore. And as an adult with the gift of perspective, I know I have to forgive myself for the way in which I went about surviving the unimaginable. There is no rule book. There wasn't one then, and there isn't one now.

I'm glad I didn't try to self-medicate with drugs or alcohol during that time. It was more out of fear of my dad's protective wrath, but it was also because my friends just didn't do those things, and the hours I spent laughing with their families around their dinner tables were better life-saving medicines than any drug I could have consumed. I did eventually develop other addictions, however, to try to soothe the pain—most notably to food, sugar, attention, and perfectionism—but these were all temporary Band-Aids.

It took me six years to accept I wasn't going to see my brother at Wall Drug in South Dakota. The body that was in the closed casket at his funeral really had been him, not just a random homeless person the authorities had pulled from the murky water to pass off as My Cedric. Sometime during college, I stopped seeing color in the world. I sunk into a deep depression in my twenties, exacerbated by the energy it took for me to stuff down my grief for so long.

My recovery process has been long and arduous. It has taken several rounds of therapy to come to terms with our family's deep dysfunction, and as a result, I have taken a few missteps,

the worst ones in the four to five years after I lost my father in 2004. I have hurt people, made grave financial errors, and allowed myself to be taken advantage of by a few opportunists. These were all attempts to fill the hole of despair within me. I wish I had learned earlier how to care for the lost little girl who experienced too much pain much too early in life. I'm still learning how to love her. I'm still healing.

When you're trapped in a dark room, you pray someone will reach in and turn on the light that will make the inky blackness disappear. When no one comes to rescue you, you stumble around with your hands flailing, desperately trying to find the elusive switch on the wall.

The King of Nonconformists

This is one of Cedric's drawings. At first, we didn't notice the flipped spear on Ced's art because we were busy looking up and not down. Look at the other masks—they are afraid of the non-conforming one (who looks uber confident). They're totally weirded out. We have news for them—we're resurrecting his nonconformist spirit. It's been there all along, like #RubySlippers!

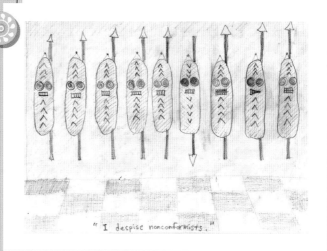

"I despise nonconformists."

I can only imagine how it felt to be trapped in Cedric's dark room—an overwhelming, lifelong struggle to exist in a world not tuned to his brilliance. Alone. Misunderstood. Longing for relief. Born before a time when seeking support and treatment was regarded as an act of courage.

As horrific as it was, losing my Big Brother eventually taught me this: stop running from pain. Instead, turn and face it—with as much help as you need to find yourself again. Close your eyes, take a deep breath, sink to the floor, and sit cross-legged in the darkness. And when you're ready, ask it to reveal what it has to teach you.

When your healing begins, it will dawn on you that you wouldn't be who you are without periods of darkness. Change one thing in your life experience, and you become someone else

walking a different path. Timing truly is everything—even when it comes to the most painful moments in life. This isn't to say that pain is justified—only that it is inevitable. The ability to endure and be transformed by pain teaches you how to show up for others who are struggling. And while they will ultimately need to find their own way, you discover you have the ability to love them through it.

Because Rainbow Unicorns Really Are the Best Unicorns

Let's hop in the Time Machine.

The decade? The '80s. The show? *Three's Company.*

In case you need a refresher or have absolutely no idea what I'm talking about, let me set the stage. *Three's Company* was a television comedy series set in Santa Monica, California. It followed the madcap adventures of Chrissy, Janet, and Jack, three roommates who lived in an apartment above their landlords, the Ropers. At that time, it was frowned upon for men and women to live together because there might be improper shenanigans going on. To get Mr. Roper to allow their mixed cohabitation, Janet told him that Jack was . . . "you know." This was done without Jack's knowledge, so for much of the show's run, they got a lot of mileage out of to Jack having to "play gay" when he was really quite straight.

Yeah . . . so THAT was my introduction to the LGBTQIA world, even though it wasn't called that back then. I laughed at Jack's antics because the live studio audience did, but in all honesty, I didn't understand why. I didn't have the words for it, and no one had ever explained it to me. Oh, I heard people using the words "light in his loafers" and "Tinkerbell" and exchanging knowing looks . . . but I was clueless. It didn't pertain to me, I thought, so I let it go as something I didn't need to think about.

This continued until I was in my late teens. I didn't know what it MEANT to be gay, and I didn't think I knew anyone who was gay, either. Sure, I heard whispered rumors about people, but no one talked about it. I just had a feeling I was supposed to think being gay was . . . bad. And somewhere along the way—either at church or a youth group event somewhere—I picked up the notion that God thought the same thing. Whew. Glad that wasn't me. Cute boys who smiled at me a certain way gave me that fluttery feeling in my chest. So did Luke Duke. Bo Brady. Johnny Castle. Maverick. Swoon! What's for supper?

In the fall of 1990, I spread my wings and flew off to Concordia College in Moorhead, Minne-

sota, a small, midwestern Lutheran school. I got myself involved in a few activities, including a worship outreach team made up of about ten of us who led youth events and services at churches in Minnesota and North Dakota a few weekends during the school year. We had a ton of fun and lots of time to bond during those long cross-country drives in our big, boxy Chevy van. We laughed. We teased each other. We took pictures. We exchanged knowing looks. We listened to each other's woes. We leaned on one another. We talked about the Big Questions of Life. We shared the Good News. We hung out. We slept in uncomfortable positions with our mouths hanging open. We harmonized. We were a great little family.

One of the guys on my team became a regular Dining Service companion of mine. We laughed over heaping bowls of cereal or commiserated over having to eat from the salad bar AGAIN because the Fried Whatever and Stewed Something Else looked gross. One day, over the course of an ordinary meal, he said he had something to tell me.

I thought for sure he was going to say he liked me, and I got nervous because I didn't think of him that way. I mean, he had thick, dark hair, and he was super funny, but my heart was currently fluttering over another guy who was on the cheerleading squad and had dazzling eyes, a quick smile, and a flirty sense of humor. And—he liked Disney as much as I did, AND he was a singer, so we were obviously a match made in heaven. Yup, I was going to have to let my worship team friend down easy. Poor guy. I didn't want to hurt his feelings. I would tell him he was super sweet, but I just wanted to stay friends.

Then—he told me he was gay. Um, what? Really? That's not what I was expecting at all. It was the first time anyone had ever come out to me. Kind of a big deal.

Do you know what I said in the next minute, without blinking an eye? I'm just gonna rip off the Band-Aid and give it to you straight: "How can you call yourself a Christian and be gay?"

The words just . . . spilled out of my mouth and landed on the tired, wobbly Dining Service table. Plop. Right there in the croutons.

He looked at me funny and stopped talking . . . and we stopped having meals together after that. Huh.

Pause: I see you. Some of you are cringing. Others of you are cheering on 1991 Carleen because what I said is perfectly acceptable to you (and maybe even necessary for his soul's survival, in your opinion). Un-pause.

I'm not going to drag this out for dramatic effect. I'm going to cut to the chase.

WHAT IN THE WORLD WAS I THINKING???

Whose voice was that coming out of my mouth? Where had I learned such a thing? Had I instantaneously forgotten he was my friend? What was I hoping to accomplish by saying that? Did I expect him to say, "Oh, you're right. Silly me. Thanks for pointing that out. Good thing you said something. Thank you, Carleen, for clearing that up. I am forever in your debt. Would you please pass the pepper?"

I didn't get it, you guys. Truly. What's worse, I had absolutely no clue how destructive and careless a statement I had made. And I didn't really give it a thought until much later in my life (like, about ten years later). It took me at least another decade to be able to plant my feet firmly on the ground, put my hands on my hips, and declare in a loud voice that I am a proud LGBTQIA ally.

I think it's important to talk about what took me so long to figure this out.

You know what it was? Religion.

Now, before you get mad, it's important for you to understand that when I say "religion," I am not talking about the pure, unconditional love that lives inside of all of us and comes to us all the way from God or whatever word you use to describe the Higher Power. Nope. I'm talking about human-created dogma that feels like it values Fear/Judgement/Separation over Love.

You know . . . Love? That thing that conquers all? The thing that remains, along with Faith and Hope (but is greater than even those two cosmically awesome things)? The thing without which you are nothing? The thing that is patient and kind? The greatest gift of all?

Yeah. THAT Love. But sometimes we get tangled up in and distracted by what I like to call The Rules.

When I was a kid, I was raised with a lot of Rules. I was supposed to know The Rules. Obey The Rules. Never question The Rules. Believe The Rules were good because they were The Rules everyone had always followed.

But what if you didn't follow The Rules? What if you wanted to talk about The Rules? What if you thought that maybe The Rules were . . . hurtful to some people? What if The Rules

seemed to go against what . . . Jesus told us to do . . . ?

Listen, child . . . you don't know what you're talking about. Just be a good little girl, have another brownie, and forget about it.

When you grow up in a dysfunctional home, obeying Rules and being a good little girl keeps you and others around you safe. That's what keeps your mother from lying on her bed and crying after another big fight. That's what makes the dinner table conversation light and happy. That's what allows you to spend more time chasing butterflies in the field instead of worrying about your brothers and your sister. That's what keeps the wild eyes and the sharp tongue away. That's what keeps you disconnected from your real self.

Your real self that's made of . . . Love. Huh.

You see, the way I reacted to my friend that day in Dining Service really had nothing to do with him and how he lived his life; instead, it had everything to do with how narrowly I had been taught to live mine. I was never encouraged to think about why I believed something. I was never taught to ask questions. I was given a script, and it was understood that I would follow it. Period. No variations. No ad-libbing. No interpretation. (Or else—but let's not talk about it, K? Shhhh.)

Then I got to know Rev. Carl Lee, one of the most gentle, loving, and accepting human beings ever to ever walk this earth. Carl was a campus pastor and the head of the counseling service at Concordia for many years. He had an absolute gift for storytelling—his Winnie-the-Pooh voice could make even the big, tough football players sniffle with homesickness during our back-to-school Wednesday Night Communion service when he read his story about missing our "Whobodies" at home. (We Cobbers looked forward to the Whobody Story tradition each fall—there was something powerful about participating

Pastor Carl Lee—an Angel with Skin to generations of Cobbers. Photo courtesy of the Concordia College Archives. (#Lini)

in a group cry and something equally powerful about committing to being Whobodies for each other at our home away from home.)

The thing about Pastor Carl you need to understand is that he loved EVERYBODY. I'm not kidding—it didn't matter who you were, where you came from, or what you'd done. He just filled you with an unconditional love that went deep into your bones. With Carl, judgement wasn't a thing. He accepted and cared for you in a way that gave you a glimpse of what heaven must be like. He made you feel like you were completely capable of loving others that way, too. He showed us what Jesus meant when he said, "Love your neighbor."

I can almost hear him saying this in his Winnie-the-Pooh voice: Everyone is loved. Jesus— God—Creator—whatever you call your Higher Power—says so. Look deep in your heart. See? Fear, hatred, and judgement just don't belong in there. That has been a done deal from the Beginning of Everything, but somehow, we've forgotten this Most Important Truth. We have to start remembering! Every perfect creation of God—meaning, every human being— deserves a beautiful, love-filled life. No exceptions.

THAT kind of love saved lives, including mine. Carl cared for me so much, I was finally able to uncurl my stiff, gnarled fingers from the six-year-old death grip I had held on grief. Carl was the one who told me it was okay to talk to Cedric because he really wasn't far away at all. Carl was the one who taught me to be a Peer Helper so I could be a Little Jesus for someone else who was hurting. Carl was the one who showed me the power of telling someone that they were important. Carl was the one who only concerned himself with one Rule (you know the one).

Pastor Carl changed the way I regarded everyone around me, even—and especially—those who were different. And as I went forth into the world, I vowed to listen, understand, and help people . . . not judge, condemn, and persecute. And as I've kept an open heart and questioned some of The Rules I grew up with, I've learned a few things. Big Things.

Let's circle back to the whole beginning of this story. This is one of those Big Things.

As a society, we've come a long way from the era of *Three's Company* when it comes to how we respond to, care for, and protect people who are part of the LGBTQIA Community. We've seen more and more people—especially in the younger generations—opening up about themselves and their orientation than ever before. Gay marriage has been legalized in our country, and individual rights have been protected. There are gay characters in films and television shows that are richly developed and so much more than tokens. We're waking up to the fact that lots of our misconceptions about the LGBTQIA community have been based on fear and myth. We understand we need to rewrite the narrative now that we know better.

But we're not where we need to be yet.

As someone who feels like pretty much everyone's sister and/or mother, I am uber-concerned there are still big pockets of judgement out there that make our LGBTQIA kidlets, friends, neighbors, coworkers, and family members feel unsafe. That's not okay. That's not following the Greatest Commandment. That's not doing what Jesus would do.

Where do we start fixing this? Our families.

People (especially kids) need their families to be there with open arms to support them unconditionally. They should never have to worry about whether they are accepted for who they truly are—how they were perfectly created. WE have to be a safe landing place. WE have to be allies. WE have to have their backs. And if anyone ever tries to hurt them because they're gay, they need to know without a DOUBT that an attacker would have to GO THROUGH THEIR FAMILIES FIRST. Period.

We can't protect them from everything forever, of course. On one level, I know they are going to have to deal with people like College Me who say stupid stuff. Some of that will happen in a world filled with humans who are also learning. On another level, I know full well there are people out there who seek to cause harm to members of the LGBTQIA Community. People I care about. People I love. Just . . . people.

We mustn't let Fear/Judgement/Separation get in the way, especially when it becomes a matter of life or death. Or life, liberty, and the pursuit of happiness. Or loving our neighbors as ourselves.

In the end, everybody is somebody's baby, and it's up to us to care for the children, no matter how old they are. So, here's my request: If you aren't in a place to offer support and love to the LGBTQIA community, then at the very least, don't add any hurt or pain. None of us started our lives that way—we accepted everyone. In the spirit of Rodgers & Hammerstein's musical *South Pacific*, you have to be taught to hate and fear.

I know it can be difficult to flip the switch because we have been programmed to Fear the Other in order to keep the team safe. But goodness . . . it's time to realize we are all on the same side, don't you think? We all have it in us to be allies. Neighbors. Life savers. Heroes. Superheroes, even.

I, for one, invite you to come and knock on my door. I've been waiting for you, so let's have coffee, chat, and move some mountains.

(To my teammate and friend from all those years ago, I am so sorry I was so clueless. Please forgive me. I'm working hard to do right by you and make our Pastor Carl smile. You already know he is. Much love to you.)

Chapter Nine

YOUR TURN!
(JOURNAL QUESTIONS)

Take some time to write about Falling in your life. You might want to use some of the prompts below or go your own direction. Do what feels natural and right for you and listen to what your writing tells you about yourself and your life.

- What messages about "falling" have you received in your life, and how have they affected you?
- Tell about a time when you had an epic "fall" and stiffened up (don't worry; we won't tell anyone, so be honest).
- Tell about a time when you had an epic "fall" and relaxed into it (we won't tell anyone about this, either, so be honest).
- Are certain "falls" easier to deal with than others?
- Which "falls" in your life have been the result of something you can control? Which ones have been the result of something over which you have no control? Do you ever try to control situations or people you really can't?
- What patterns do you notice about times that you have "fallen"?
- Who are the people who stand with you and help you? What do they do for you?
- When have you positively helped others? Or, when could you positively help others in the future? What was that like/what could that be like for you?
- My biggest "a-ha" related to this section is . . . because . . .
- I hope to . . .
- I am grateful for . . .

Rule #2

_____

_____

_____

_____

_____

_____

_____

_____

_____

_____

_____

_____

_____

_____

_____

_____

_____

Chapter Ten

Idea #1: Grounding (aka Get Outside!)

Where did you spend most of your time when you were a kid? If you're like a lot of people, you just screamed, "OUTSIDE!" in your head (or maybe even out loud). Whether our parents told us to get outside the minute they saw us sitting on the couch or whether we dreamed of nothing else but freeing ourselves from the confines of our houses, being outside used to be a huge part of our lives. It felt, well, natural, didn't it? Then something else came along and interrupted all that: responsibility. Something else did too: shoes (even the cute ones).

There is recent research as to whether the practice of "grounding" or "earthing" is actually beneficial to the human body. What do those terms mean? Andrew Weil, M.D., notes that proponents of grounding claim that as modern society has progressed, our connection to the earth has regressed, and because we aren't exchanging electrons with our Mother, we're getting sicker and more stressed out.[2] And when you add the effects of the electromagnetic fields that are everywhere now that we're a tech-crazy bunch, well, no wonder we can't sleep. Weil cautions we need more high-quality research to know if grounding really makes a difference, especially when it comes to our bank accounts (there are lots of products out there to combat all that negative electricity around you).

As we stated before, we aren't experts.

But we don't need research to tell us that we feel better when we take time to tango with Terra Firma. Right? Other than critters and allergies, is there anything that should hold us back from occasionally taking off our shoes and socks to let the grass tickle our toes, to dangle our feet in the water, or to leave footprints in the sand? Absolutely not!

We are the ones holding ourselves back from this because A.) we think we don't have time, B.) we think it's for kids, or C.) we're more worried about tracking dirt into the house than taking a few minutes to center ourselves.

All that is bunk. Get rid of it and get outside. Whatever it is you like to do in the wilds—go do it. Lisa keeps a pot of sand in her house and puts her feet in it when she just can't stand it anymore. Carleen used to put her feet in the mud on the side of the road as soon as she wasn't in danger of freezing them in the spring. And both of us "SQUEEEEEEEE!!!" when we are in our gardens. We don't even care if we ruin our occasional manicures.

Perfectly feathered hair and the cool jersey that someone had left soaking wet on the dock. I mean, someone needed to give it a home! And that might be my Motley Crüe bandana around my waist. (#Lili)

We can't say with all clinical certainty that grounding truly reduces inflammation in the body—but big deal. Every human being who breathes knows that slowing down to smell the roses (the real kind in the garden, not the artificial air freshener type) brings us into the present moment and makes us feel better. Less stressed. More apt to smile at people. Happy. It also doesn't take an expert to know that reducing stress and strain on the body reduces cortisol levels, which is one of the best things you can do for yourself because cortisol breaks down all kinds of things. So why not try it? There's a little girl inside you who is just DYING to get out and play again, so take a few minutes and care for her. Don't forget to breathe deeply. Breathe again. And again. Yaaaaassssss.

Upside down glasses, an attempt at feathering, and a fake Members Only jacket from the J.C. Penney catalog. (#Lini)

Grounding (The Imagination Version)

Okay, so maybe it's forty below, and you just can't bear the thought of putting your feet in the snow. Or maybe you're in a meeting, and your client would look at you sideways if you started peeling off your shoes and tights. Maybe you really DON'T want to deal with the mess.

Fine—we've got you. You can ground yourself in your mind, and it only takes a few minutes of visualization.

If you haven't done a lot of meditation, this might sound weird, but trust us—it works. All you have to do is close your eyes (if you can), take a deep breath, and visualize roots growing from the bottom of your feet. Let those tendrils of feet-tree goodness work their way down through the floor in your mind, all the way to the dirt underneath whatever structure you're in and beyond. Picture them going down, down, down into the earth until they find some nice, steady, solid rocks. Picture your roots wrapping themselves around those rocks and giving them a hug. Doesn't that feel good? Yes! Those roots will whisper to you, "Okay, we've got you now. Everything is all secure. Nothing can knock you over. We've got your back."

Ahhhhhh . . . there you go. Look at you, you graceful being, you—handling everything like a tree. Just remember that trees with strong roots are able to sway and bend through the worst of storms before righting themselves again in the sunshine (which always returns—actually, it didn't go anywhere—it was just hidden temporarily behind the storm).

Idea #2: Animal Therapy

Animals have tremendous power to bring us joy and to heal us. They can turn the biggest, tattooed dude into a doting doggy dad. They can make a hurried lawn-mowing mom (Lisa) stop and make a little hut for a frog with a hurt leg. They can walk into hospitals, nursing homes, schools, and therapy offices and bring comfort to everyone around them.

From the more traditional choices of dogs and cats to the less traditional hermit crab (hermit crabs are VERY social) or goat, animals have been enriching our lives for as long as we have been appreciating and domesticating them. They can be incredibly intuitive and sensitive. My dog Sandy used to lick my emo, boy-driven tears away when I was a teenager (not because they were salty, but because she was empathizing with me . . . was too shut up). Our dog, Buddy, knew when my father-in-law was very ill, and he sat on his lap, trying to heal him. My cat, Dakota, peed on my school bag (think one-hundred tinted-yellow Spanish exams) one day. I got upset and yelled at him. He got upset and threw up.

Kiddo begs me to go to PetSmart and the Humane Society so that she can pet #AllTheKittiesAndPuppies. She has always loved animals, ever since she was a teeny, tiny girl. She runs with arms wide open at any dog, no matter the size. She was able to catch and hold animals that no one else was able to catch or hold. At eight years old, she led the orneriest

pony at horse camp when no one else could.

Why are children so drawn to animals? Is it because they feel animals understand them more than adults? Is it because they give them unconditional love? Is it because they never hesitate to play and never complain? Is it because they are closer to their size? Is it because they can always count on them to lend an ear? Why do we sometimes lose that as adults? There is a reason therapy dogs and therapy horses exist, right? Pet therapy, whether formal or informal, is not just for The Littles! Even watching birds on the deck is soothing and healing for the soul.[3]

Therapy dogs provide emotional support to sick and injured people in many settings. According to www.pawsforpeople.org, therapy dogs have a documented positive effect on our physical and mental health.[4] Being with them can lower blood pressure, improve cardiovascular health, help us release calming oxytocin, diminish physical pain, and help us relax, all of which can help reduce the amount of medication a patient takes. On top of that (as every pet owner knows), therapy dogs lift our spirits; comfort us; help us communicate; decrease boredom, loneliness, depression, and anxiety; and increase our sense of belonging and community. They can even help kids overcome speech and emotional disorders.

All this recovery goodness comes wrapped up in a ball of fluffy puppy goodness! If you are an animal person dealing with stress from #AllTheThings or from #BigThings, it might not hurt to find therapists in your area who have these extra-special companions.

The first therapy dog that I (Lisa) ever met was a lab named Jenga. Because he has arthritis, doing the normal service dog stuff wore him down over time, so he discovered a new career working one-on-one with people during therapy sessions. He is a bit of a nervous guy, so he also has a lot of empathy for clients with anxiety.

I met him during a rough moment in time for our family. We were switching schools, and while Kiddo was on board with it, it was still a pretty difficult change. Once, while meeting with the counselor, Kiddo put her head into her hoodie and refused to come out. Then Jenga walked in. Unable to control myself, I exclaimed, "PUPPERS!" That was all it took! Kiddo popped her head out, and she and Jenga have been BFFs ever since.

Jenga put everyone at ease, whether it was Kiddo alone, Kiddo and me, or the whole fam. My child, the Animal Whisperer, discovered quickly she could lie on him, a privilege extended to no one else. It was the beginning of a beautiful relationship; he has been a source of calm in any storm. Jenga doesn't ask questions; Jenga just knows. He knows who needs what and when they need it. Every time.

Our therapist left the program Kiddo attended, and it was a month and a half before we could see her and Jenga in their new practice. We seriously mourned—it was awful. Our therapist is the best we ever worked with, but the two together are a team that can't be beat. We love them both dearly and recommend animal-assisted therapy as a wonderful strategy to help make life's wipeouts more graceful.

Idea #3: Be Still

One of the best things we can do to fall more gracefully is turn inward. We don't suggest you totally withdraw from the world—we're talking about simply carving out time to disconnect from the craziness, still your mind, and refocus so you can make good decisions about what to do next. There's no need to agonize over a decision because the wisdom we seek is already within, waiting for us to slow down enough to become aware of it.

Some people call this prayer, some people call it meditation, and some people may have another name for it altogether. There are many, many belief systems out there, and we respect that you may be grounded in a specific tradition. Do whatever works for you!

However you practice Being Still, here are some tips we want to throw out:

1. Pay attention to how you feel. Notice if your body is giving signals that it's under stress. Is your breathing shallow and quick? Do you have pain somewhere like your gut or shoulders? Do you feel like you're in quicksand? Are you about to boil over with anger? Do you feel like you're getting smaller and smaller, and your "emotional stuff" is filling in the space around you? Are you snapping at people? Are you eating the sixth chocolate chip cookie after also eating four spoonfuls of dough? (coughCarleencough) Is your mind starting to race and perseverate on #AllTheBadThings?

    More than likely, you know your body's way of telling you it needs help. If you feel like you don't know, try tuning in more to see if you can hear it talk to you—or if you're brave enough, ask someone you trust if they notice any behavioral patterns that might indicate you need to listen to the messages your body is sending you. (We know this is risky if you aren't ready to hear this, but it can help. Trust is key.)

2. When you get the signal your body needs you to be still, switch into Big Sister mode. Tell

yourself, It is okay to take care of myself. It is okay to be still so I can fill my tanks of resiliency back up. I will be a stronger human if I do this for myself. I will be a better person in my loved ones' lives if I take care of myself.

3. As best you can, create some mental/emotional space around you. If you are in the middle of something, try a quick, deep breathing technique. If you are in a place where you can safely retreat for a while, do that. Go into your bedroom, shut the door, close the curtains, lie down, and close your eyes. Or lean back in your chair for a bit. Or stretch out on a yoga mat. Or even put your head down on your desk. (We've done that. #DontJudge.)

4. Actively tune your attention to something that will bring you some peace and calm. For example, you might:

    a. **Repeat a positive mantra.** It might be something as simple as, "I am okay; I am loved; I am not alone." Whatever you choose to repeat, keep it positive. Do not say something like, "I suck. I am terrible. Everything is falling apart. I'm drowning." If you start going down that path (and let's be real, we've all done it), gently bring yourself back around to words that lift you up.

    b. **Pray.** If you are a person who feels connected to a Higher Power, have a conversation with that Power. Focus on the power of that conversation. Think about how good it feels to talk with a trusted friend about your stuff. Your Higher Power IS about as trusted a friend as you can have. Put your questions out there. Call out for help. Voice what you are thankful for. But then—listen.

    c. **Meditate.** There are some wonderful meditation videos on YouTube that can lead you through progressive relaxation techniques that will help you refocus your thoughts and relax deeply.

    Take the time to figure out which style of meditation appeals to you. Do you like a female or male voice? Do you like it to be straightforward, or do you like something a little more "out there" and pixie-dusty? Do you want soothing music playing during the meditation or just a voice? There are even recordings out there that have binaural beats, which are frequencies aimed at relaxing certain parts of the brain and getting it to release feel-good chemicals.

    Test drive a few models, and if they don't feel right, move on to another one. Eventually you'll find something that rings your bell. This is one of the best things about technology—we have so many resources at our fingertips!

If you make meditation a nightly practice, you will likely discover you sleep more soundly. Just be sure to turn off autoplay so you aren't woken up by another, less soothing video (like something from your favorite '80s hair band or Beethoven's Fifth).

d. **Focus on gratitude.** Turning our attention to what we are thankful for is sometimes enough of a mental/emotional reset to get us through a hard time. A good way to do this is keeping a gratitude journal. It doesn't have to be fancy or lengthy—you can even just keep a bullet point list on your phone if that works best for you. The point is to anchor your thoughts to the good in your life. And it doesn't matter if everything you write down feels little. Size matters not. Just ask Yoda.

I was visiting Dan in Los Angeles after he moved out there. I used that yellow shaker sweater as a weapon. (#Lili)

e. **Notice beauty**. This works well when you are in the middle of something else and can't exactly sequester yourself. Hey—look at that cool beam of light coming out of the clouds. That color of blue really looks good on everyone, doesn't it? I like the saying on that T-shirt. Look at how tall and majestic that tree is! That puppy dog over there is a professional tail-wagger. My favorite song is playing in the elevator. I love the architecture of this building. Look at that flower growing in the concrete. Whatever it is—if it's beautiful to you, love it up. Let it into your soul to remind you there are things all around you that have the power to lift you up.

I felt like all that and a bag of chips in that Hawaii suit at Lake Vermilion (a rare moment of confidence). This was well before the cellulite came in. (#Lini)

Idea #4: Practice Forgiveness (Including Yourself)

Let's face it; forgiveness can be difficult, depending on the situation and the depth of the hurt we experience. It's such a big subject, whole books have been written about it, and it is one of the central cornerstones of most major belief systems.

Some hurts you just have to brush off, like getting flipped off for having the audacity to zipper merge properly during the morning rush hour. Something like that is not worth the stress, right? Of course, you might get mad in the moment, but holding onto it for any length of time is like drinking poison and expecting the other person to die (as the popular saying goes). Nope. Not worth it.

Other things are harder to get over, however, especially if we are hurt by someone we trust (especially if they are supposed to LOVE us or at least LIKE us). A partner says something cutting during an argument that you SWEAR you've had at least fifty times before. A friend puts your business out on Front Street after she PROMISED she would keep it in confidence. Family members surprise you with their Mr. Hyde side (when you believed they were the Dr. Jekyll type). A trusted coworker throws you under the bus (and then tells it to back up as soon as you clear the tires).

Yeah. That's sucky.

I (Carleen) can get easily triggered by this kind of hurt—a response I can trace back to the stress in my childhood home. ("You spend most of your adulthood recovering from your childhood" is a saying that makes you feel justified when you're the kid and terrible when you're the parent.)

My dad was, in a word, controlling. He also yelled—a LOT—sometimes about the littlest things. You never wanted to screw up in any way and endure the Wrath of Morris (especially with a vehicle of his, which was an extension of his body). The Wrath intensified after he was diagnosed with lupus and put on a high-powered steroid that saved his life, but also made his fire burn with the intensity of seven suns (we didn't know that Prednisone Rage was a thing until years later).

He was accomplished at controlling people in other ways too. When I was little and got "out of line" in the least bit (which wasn't much, because I was a good kid), my dad would say in a low, growly, shame-on-you voice, "Do you know what you're turning into? A spoiled BRAT." I didn't know WHAT that was, but I was absolutely terrified of being one. That might sound a little humorous, but it made me SUPER anxious. When I was older and did something like, I don't know, disagree with him, he'd pull this one out: "I should have never been a father." Oof. That makes a kid feel loved. And having to scream into your pillow while your parents fought or your siblings got a tongue-lashing? Equally awesome.

These examples should give you a feel for the amount of cortisol my brain was bathing in. It took a long time to untangle the knots. It also took me quite a while to forgive him.

When did I start forgiving him? Halloween of 2004. I will never forget the look on his face as he sat in his hospital bed, struggling to breathe with lungs that only had 10 percent of their capacity, thanks to a fungal infection that had taken hold because of his compromised immune system. He looked so small and forlorn in his gown. I said to him, "Dad . . . are you scared?" He nodded his head, his eyes getting bigger with every labored breath. All I could do in that moment was say, "Dad . . . you're going to be okay. Take it easy. Let the doctors help you. I love you, Dad. It's going to be all right." Before me sat a frightened little boy who needed his mother—and it dawned on me in that moment that maybe that's who he always had been, even when he was raging. That was the last conversation he had with anyone in our family. When we came back from dinner an hour later, he had been intubated and sedated and would never regain consciousness.

So . . . does extending forgiveness to someone excuse what they have done to you? Does it mean that you are required to say, "That's okay?" Absolutely not, and we say this as people who have been wronged—sometimes terribly—AND as people who have wronged others—sometimes terribly.

One of the most poignant definitions of forgiveness we've ever seen comes from our Soul Sister, Oprah, as she reflected on her 25-year experience as the host of *The Oprah Winfrey Show*. In a segment from Oprah's Lifeclass, she summed up one of the most important lessons she'd learned from a guest: "Forgiveness is giving up the hope that the past could be any different."

Take a minute and reflect on the power of that statement. Hope is a good thing, right? We aren't ever supposed to give up hope, right? Usually—yes! We are all about hope—there is not enough of it in this world, and sometimes it is the only thing that gets us through a tough spot.

What Oprah is saying, however, is that hope gets tangled up when we try to use it backwards. It is only meant to be used with eyes facing forward. And if you keep looking at something hurtful in the past, then you are being held in place—a prisoner to an emotion that is not going to rewrite history, no matter how many times you try to make it.

Once a moment is past—in any situation—what's done is done. There is no changing the fact it happened. Not a single one of us has a time machine (at least, not yet), and there is no undoing of anything, ever. Brooding and gnashing your teeth will not change history one iota. There

is also no guarantee that perseverating on a negative situation will have an effect on the person who hurt you, either—especially if that person is not around to witness how hurt you are.

So, you have a choice to make. You can either choose to dwell on it, or you can choose to accept it happened and move on. This doesn't mean you can't hurt. It doesn't mean what happened to you was justified. It doesn't mean you have to excuse anything. By forgiving, you are choosing not to be held prisoner anymore. You are choosing not to absorb stress chemicals anymore. You are choosing to open yourself up to healing so you can get on with the business of growing and living and helping others. And maybe—just maybe—you are choosing to understand that hurt people hurt others, and what happened to you may have been fueled by deep pain you are not aware of. Explanations for behavior—not excuses—do exist.

I don't know who hurt my dad so deeply that he would turn his pain on others, especially his family, but his experience had to be pretty bad. And it's not a stretch to say he was probably struggling with a mental illness of some sort. You just don't treat people that way and NOT have something going on.

I do know I am grateful I had the chance to tell him I loved him before he went unconscious—and telling him that did NOT in any way excuse that he was a difficult parent much of the time. And as Matthew's dad and I sat with him early on Thanksgiving morning as he lay dying, I kept telling him that he was loved. I held his hand. I told him that I forgave him. I thanked him for showing his love for us the best way he could. Working hard to support us, even when he was in pain. Making sure our cars were running smoothly and wouldn't leave us on the side of the road. Taking us for boat rides and pulling us expertly on waterskis. Coming to every concert and parade. Offering advice.

My dad died peacefully just after 7:00 a.m. . . . . and I let go of the lion's share of my hurt. And the rest of it? I'm still cleaning out the residual stuff. It's like dust—it gets into everything.

Okay . . . let's change gears. What happens when YOU'VE been the one doing the hurting? We've all wrestled with this to some extent . . . Lord, have we wrestled. And if you haven't made a big mistake yet, you will. It is part of the gig called Being Human.

Here's the deal: if you can, you should apologize if you have hurt someone or done something you aren't proud of. Yes, you should try to make amends. Yes, you absolutely MUST change your behavior to show you are truly sorry (it is not okay to say, "My bad," and then turn around and do it again). But it is crucial to understand there is a huge difference between saying, "I did a bad thing," and saying, "I am a bad person." (More on this in section 3's #SpinGold chapter, if you want to look ahead.)

Part of the process of changing your behavior, Soul Sisters, involves allowing yourself to be an imperfect human surrounded by other imperfect humans. To move forward, you must allow your imperfection to be a part of the story of Messy You Learning How to Be a Better Human, for better or for worse. Then you absolutely must allow yourself to BE that better version of yourself who is capable of doing good in the world. Otherwise you run the risk of causing more hurt, either to someone else or to yourself. You must stop the cycle, and if you need help doing so, reach out to those who can help you.

Fall if you must, but try to do it with some grace based in love. Just by existing, you have just as much worth as anyone else. Not more, not less. Just as much. So, love yourself throughout whatever you're going through. You are not the only human being to make a mistake—what matters is what you do with what you learn from the experience.

And don't worry about what anyone else thinks or says about you—their response is all about them, and you can't control what anyone else thinks or does. The only person you can control is yourself.

So, take as many breaths as you need to steady yourself and give up the hope the past can be any different. Then move on and use that sh*tty experience as fertilizer to grow something beautiful.

Idea #5: Find Your Team

We REALLY love vintage images of women waterskiing. Why do we love them? Let us count the ways! First, of course, is because it is well-established that midcentury is our thing. (MAYBE we once lived in the midcentury! Who knows! #PixieDust!) Second—it's waterskiing, so that goes without saying we'd like it.

If you really look closely at these vintage images, you'll see there's a certain confidence in these ladies because they are in. It. Together. They are each doing their own thing, but they are also aware of one another. They know any movement by one will affect the other members, positively or negatively. They respect each other's space, they don't ski over each other, and they make each other look goooood.

We also imagine they take turns leading the team, and one of them does not outshine the

Summer of '69 (#Lili)

Our Midcentury Parental Units

"1950s America . . . an amorous affair with the molecular which would ultimately shift into a universal apocalyptic dread unprecedented in human history. North American paradox at its best."[5]

Ooooo, child. We want the promise of having it ALL figured out, and then we fall apart. You can be ALL THESE THINGS—EXTRA AND MESSED UP. It's okay. You're okay. It's all fine. Oops, now it isn't. That's okay. HAHAHAHAHAHA! No WONDER Midcentury Modern Atomic is our thing . . .

Those glasses. Those smiles. That iconic "just married" photo. (#Lini)

other. If someone loses balance, they do everything they can to steady her again. If a wipeout happens, they assess the situation and decide whether they can get up and try again or whether they need to take a break. And when it's time to do something fabulous, they each bring awesome strengths and talents that lift and magnify the group.

Plus . . . look at all those kick-ass vintage swimsuits!

(Speaking of clothing, we want to pause here and talk about something quick, #KK?)

We guess a bunch of you have a few of those cutesy shirts with clever words on them in your closet. We do too, and we think they're quite #EXTRA. Sayings like #SquadGoals and #BrideTribe seem to be all the rage these days—just dial up Instagram or troll the women's section at many stores, and you'll see what we mean.

Now, the sentiment of these shirts is good: Girl Power! We're strong! We support each other! Right? But even though they are kinda catchy-cute, the words "Squad" and "Tribe" are actually not the most culturally respectful words to use. ("Squad" has its origins in African American Vernacular English, and "Tribe" comes directly from Native/First Peoples culture.)

As Soul Sisters who always err on the side of respect, we need to avoid cultural appropriation. This is when the dominant culture adopts only selective aspects of a minority culture without grappling with what it means to be part of that culture—especially when it comes to their struggles. If it's hard to get your head around what that really means, a simple example would be a white model wearing a headdress—something that is sacred in Native culture and only to be worn by adult male leaders. Basically, it's not cool to borrow parts of someone's identity for a few hours and then give it back because you can.

People-Who-Look-Like-Us, we know the line between cultural appropriation and cultural appreciation can be blurry, especially when certain catchy phrases are all the rage, and you have trouble keeping up with where everything comes from! Our best advice? Keep your eyes and ears open. Search the InterWebs. Talk to people of color about it. And when you become aware of it, follow the advice of our love, Maya Angelou: "When you know better, do better."

(Also, sometimes the words "Squad" and "Tribe" feel a little exclusionary. Like, "You can't be a part of our club." Yeah, that doesn't feel good . . .)

Having a group of women around you to support you, lift you up, and give you a #LlamaKick or a #FlamingoThwack when you need one is uber important. We wanted to call this special group something spunky, but it had to be something culturally neutral that doesn't smack of *Mean Girls*, if you know what we mean. Everyone must feel like she can use the name and feel good about it and herself, no matter who she is or where she comes from. To make sure this happens, we're going to fall back on Cedric's Waterskiing Metaphor and go with . . . TEAM. Sure, it's a little generic, but we can make it AWESOME and make everyone feel welcome and equal at the same time.

I haaaaaate being cold. I was trying SO hard to stay outside to write. (#Lili)

Blooper Reels All the Way

The thing about social media is that it's all about the highlight reel. This is SO not us! No matter how big a trainwreck is happening (and we're stuck with our blooper reel on repeat),
#TheCamerasKeepRollingWithUs
#SorryForWhatWeSaid
WhenWeNeededCakesAndTacos
#WhatIsUpWithAllTheRetrogrades

One of my 6:00 a.m. "State of Affairs" selfies for Lisa. Thank God for Dry Shampoo. (#Lini)

So. Hi, Team! Let's talk about #Teamness. #Team-o-rama. #Teamy-Team-Team.

As we've said before, we all want to be connected to others. Some of us are lucky and have friendships that go WAY back, maybe even to junior high or elementary school. Some of us have formed friendships at work, in a club or organization, or because our kids are in the same activities. Some of us live in neighborhoods where people have regular bonfires, holiday parties, or standing invitations to come over for a beer and some cornhole on the day of the Big Game. If this is you—we are super happy for you. Everyone deserves that kind of friendship. Everyone deserves a great team. Everyone deserves to have a soft place to land when life gets tough. Everyone deserves a group to clink glasses with when there's something awesome to celebrate.

But we Women in the Middle sometimes discover it's harder to make and maintain friendships that are as deep as the ones we had when we were younger—before marriage, before kids, before we saw the passage of decades, and before #AllTheThings. We know that as a result, there are MANY women out there who feel alone. If this feels familiar, know we've been there, too. We've sat and wondered, "What's wrong with me? Am I ever going to have a friend like So-and-So ever again? Am I doomed to a life of forced isolation?"

You aren't alone. There is a WHOLE GALAXY of Positive Sisters orbiting all around you. On one hand, it's all about finding them, but on the other, it's about making yourself known as one, too. One way to do this is to have shared experiences—like bunco, book club, mom groups, $5 Tuesday girls' movie night, exercise classes, community ed groups, faith communities, social action groups, and so on.

Social media, for all its ills, can also be a positive way into a team. There are Facebook groups for literally everything these days, so think of what brings you joy, search it up, and see who's out there. Reach back to them. Suggest meeting to have coffee or go for a group walk or something else fun and low-key. A friend of Lisa's told us about Bumble BFF, which is basically the friend version of a dating app. This might sound . . . unusual, but hey — give it a try, especially if you have recently moved and want to get connected.

Listen, we know it can be tough when your to-do list is a mile long and you feel like a zombie from lack of sleep, but even a little bit of reaching out can make a difference. And remember one of the most important pieces of advice our mothers likely gave all of us: be yourself. Be authentically and unapologetically you. Leave the filters to Insta.

Behold the Christmas Llamas

Lisa: Do you have Christmas llamas like these?

Carleen: . . . aren't those . . . reindeer?

Lisa: No. They are definitely Christmas llamas.

Carleen: *blinks*

Lisa: Kris had one too!!! It was a sign that I had found the right guy! Who else would have a Christmas llama in the bottom of a Christmas bin? *mumbles to self* . . . totally a Christmas llama.

I didn't know that anyone else had a Christmas llama until I was digging through Kris's Christmas bins after we were married. When you find your Christmas llama, hold on tight! (#Lili)

Lisa: I'm at a point where I need to control my larger environment and I need to do it with like-minded women. Women with whom I have an ironclad pact about our values, and how we live our values. A place where ego and negativity get stamped out. The older I get the less I can deal with that sh*t. Life is way too short. Get out of my face with it. Get gone.

My team mentality is always include, never exclude. I have been "teaming" for the last five years without even realizing it. Family and friends are so important to me, and my adult life has been fraught with upheaval regarding me having my own family. After my second marriage dissolved, I didn't know #WTH to do. I was exhausted, and I was angry. But, as always, I listened to my mom, and I kept an open heart. It took me four years to find my forever guy, but I found him. So, one thing that has become very important to me is hosting Christmas Day in our home. It is the one time every year I can bring both sides of my family together.

This was modeled for me at family gatherings when I was little. This is how I was raised. Family from all sides were included at any holiday. And if anybody needed a place to be, they were welcome. Fast forward and picture this: My mother and my mother-in-law. My father and my father-in-law. My sister, my sister-in-law, and my soul sister, Kathy. My brother, my husband, and my husband's best friend, Shawn. Lisa is in her happy place. THIS is what I teach my daughter. THIS is how my team rolls. Now, several years later, we have lost my father-in-law, and my parents live in Arizona. But everyone else

can always count on Christmas Day at our house.

Another thing that brings me Pixie Dust Joy is the power of having Soul Sisters from different areas of my life gather at our oily convention in Salt Lake City. We've done this for two years now. It has happened organically, but any gathering of my Forever People and my Soul Sisters at such an amazing event makes me go SQUEEEEEEEE!!! #ThingsThatMakeYouGoSqueeeeee #SisterhoodOfTheTravellingDiffuser

Hard and fast rule: we are women who build each other up. Under no circumstance will we tear each other down. We are adults. We don't give hints; we speak our mind—respectfully and with integrity and honor. And we include, include, include.

My Cissy and my nieces/little sisters: Alissa, Joy, and Amy. The Sisu Sisters! (#Lini)

Carleen: I've come to deeply appreciate the strong women in my family. Growing up, I was surrounded by them but didn't really understand what a gift that was until I started adulting myself. Grandmas, aunties, older cousins, my Cissy, neighbors, church ladies— they all showed me what it meant to work hard, to get through tough times, and still get dinner on the table.

Now there is a new generation of strong family women to learn from—my nieces. Even though I am technically Auntie Carleen, they feel more like my little sisters (let's be real—sometimes they are like big sisters). They are teaching me about a whole other layer of strength as they make their way through the world. There's a whole other book just waiting to be written about all these beautiful women—the team I was born into; the team I wish I had living closer to me. That is one thing a lot of us are missing these days in our spread-out, busy-busy world.

When it comes to friends, there have been many women with whom I have connected deeply—I could name at least twenty people right off the top of my head—but for a multitude of reasons, some of us have cycled in and out of each other's lives.

Some of the cycling has been natural. Life moves you in different directions based on who you marry, what your kids are doing, the job you have, where you live, the personal struggles you're dealing with, and so forth. Some of those friendships come back around, but some don't—and that is the way of things. You bless one another for one season or for many.

Even though I know this logically, sometimes my anxiety tells me a different story—like, maybe I did something to make the cycling happen. Maybe these women decided I wasn't the kind of person they wanted to be friends with. This is difficult because you don't know if there was something you could have done better to keep these friendships going . . . or if you, yourself, are flawed. Maybe I was the one to drop the ball by not answering texts, picking up the phone, or making enough time for friends because I was too focused on my "stuff."

Some of the cycling happened, however, because I decided it was better for my well-being to move on from some friendships. These were the most heartbreaking choices to make because they felt like a death—and I was the one that removed the life support (I feel bad, even though I know I am healthier as a result of such a decision).

If you are lucky, you have that one girlfriend (or several) you can call about anything—the one who would help you bury a dead body first and ask questions later, metaphorically speaking. ;) Sometimes you go through a dry spell, though, which is lonely. I am grateful that this Cosmic Soul Sister Thing has happened, especially at a time in my life when everything is changing. And I am equally grateful for the women who have stuck with me through the good times and bad— especially those who have seen me at my worst and still love me anyway. #ThatsLove (and you know who you are).

Brain Farts Happen, So Make the Best of 'Em

Carleen: Glamper Coffee—a drop of peppermint oil, some Truvia, and some almond milk from that carton in the back of the fridge. Wait, what? What did I just pour in there? CHICKEN BROTH? Oh, for . . . damn it. Welp, don't wanna waste the peppermint. Bottoms up! Chicken Coffee it is!

Lisa: Oh, hahaha. That's funny! I'm laughing WITH you, Sister. *three days later* OH, BLOODY HELL. I literally just did the same thing with my smooooooothie . . .

Carleen: Details, details, details. #SometimesYouJustDrink TheChickenCoffee

What I have learned through it all is that all these relationships have shaped me. All these women are woven into my fabric. All of them have taught me things that have made me a better version of myself. We were meant to find each other exactly when we did. And if the friendship came to a close, it is important to remember the good that came of it and not dwell on the loss.

We thought we'd end this strategy with one of our Early Morning Ping Sessions (which translates to us texting about the book first thing in the morning while hiding under the covers so as not to wake our sleeping partners). (Sorry, Scott and Kris . . .) We tried to make it an actual poem, but it's better in its original form.

Carleen: I think I might feel a poem coming on. Sometimes I think that there are behaviors to recognize that are cool. This is totally stream of consciousness thinking . . .

Lisa: Ohhhhhhh . . . Hmmmmmmm . . . Interesting . . .

Carleen: How about the definition of a soul sister??

Lisa: Yes!

Carleen: Like, how you know that the #Llamicles are lined up properly?

Lisa: Twinkling at the same frequency?

Lisa: An immediate understanding

Lisa: Riding the same wave

Carleen: Saying, "That must be so hard"

Lisa: Empathy and compassion

We had a ball doing a photo shoot with Kiddo as our official photographer. She didn't mess around (but we did!).

Carleen: Lifting up instead of tearing down

Lisa: Normally a hugger

Lisa: Literally never turning down

Carleen: Assuming positive intentions

Carleen: Swift, loving kicks in the rear when necessary

We had a chance to hear Glennon Doyle (and Abby Wambach was there, too!) speak in 2018. We got a little #FanGirly. #SorryNotSorry

Lisa: Motivator extraordinaire

Lisa: Always gives a helping hand

Carleen: Forgiving

Lisa: Loving

Carleen: Asking, what might be behind that behavior?

Lisa: Emanator of light

Lisa: Seeks to understand

Carleen: Believing people when they say they need a break or a boundary

Carleen: Laughter

Lisa: Emanator? (Is that a word?)

Carleen: Yes

Lisa: Regarding break or boundary: believing without question and respecting the choice

Carleen: Sunshine on a cloudy day

Carleen: But sometimes cloudy with a chance of meatballs

Lisa: Farts glitter

Carleen: Dream encourager

Lisa: Open

Lisa: Growth mindset

Lisa: Flexible

Carleen: Agree to disagree with love always

Lisa: Always welcoming and inclusive

Lisa: Elevating

Lisa: Goes out of their way to be inclusive

Carleen: Patient

Lisa: Edifying

Carleen: Oooooo!

Carleen: Checks in

Lisa: Believes that people are basically good and seeks to find the good in all

Carleen: We can organize all of this under Love and Fear

Lisa: Squeee!!!

Lisa: That is a short high-pitched one

Lisa: PERFECT

The Shaffner family loves John Prine. We have seen him together a few times. This photo was taken after one of his concerts in Minneapolis. (#Lili)

Carleen: Like The Characteristics of a Love-Based Team and Those of a Fear-Based Team

Lisa: For those of a Fear-Based Team, we could simply put "the opposite of the characteristics of a Love-Based Team"

Carleen: TOTALLY!!! We all help each other sort out the pieces

Lisa: And I think that many many many many many many many many women feel lost

Lisa: Because they don't have a team

Lisa: This needs to be the rule

Lisa: Every single woman needs a team—a place to belong and feel included

Carleen: We must lift each other up. Make connections. Be the Belonging Place.

Lisa: It is astounding to me how many lost women there are—we hear about it

Lisa: By looking at the #ExtraKids in our lives, and the #ExtraDoggos, we can be reminded of what it feels like to not be so controlled by fear and pain

Lisa: People have acquaintances, but you have to have people you can fart in front of

Lisa: #ZeroApologies

Lisa: #YouCanFartInFrontOfMe

Carleen: #DivineFeminineFarts

So . . . GO TEAM, and remember that the magic happens when talented and lovely individuals get together and MAKE the magic happen. And when the atomic bombs of life hit, it's important to be fallout shelters for each other.

Idea #6: Oils We Like for This

Lavender
Patchouli
Frankincense
Sacred Frankincense
Bergamot
Geranium

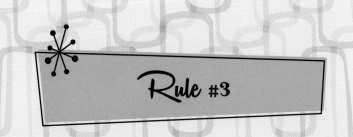

Rule #3

WHEN YOU FALL,
LET GO OF THE ROPE.

Chapter Eleven

THE KEY WORD IS "WHEN"

Dear Lovelies,

A-hem.

"Let it go . . . let it gooo-ooooo . . ." We can't have a Rule of Life as illustrated by Waterskiing that refers to "letting go" without giving a nod to your favorite earworm, now, can we? You're welcome.

Take two. Derp.

We established in the Wipeout section that humans fall down throughout their lives—from their first, go-get-'em steps as toddlers to all sorts of horrific wipeout possibilities as adults. We also talked about the power of forgiveness—self forgiveness and other forgiveness—as a powerful way to fall gracefully.

If we KNOW we're going to fall because we're human, and falling is just part of the gig we signed up for, why do we keep holding onto the rope? We know letting go means

Matching Elmer Fudd hats! (#Lili)

Helping Matthew find humor while waiting for surgery on his broken arm. (#SnowboardWipeout) Just so you know, barf bags have names—this one is Alberto. (#Lini)

the falling will stop sooner than later. Letting go means maybe we won't hit that big rock over there that is just WAITING to give us a traumatic brain injury. Letting go sooner means we can recover faster and get ourselves back up on our skis feeling like we are GLORIOUS GOD-DESSES IN CHARGE OF LIFE, THE UNIVERSE, AND EVERYTHING once again.

So . . . what in the world are we thinking? Why do we maintain a complete death grip on the handle and continue to take a faceful of water? Maybe the key word to consider in Rule of Life #3 is "When."

Listen, Soul Sisters . . . we WILL FALL. That is a 100 percent guaranteed fact. Sometimes, though, we think we are the exception to the rule. We don't believe it will happen. We're perfectionists. We don't allow ourselves the grace to fall. We think once we fall a certain way, we'll be smart enough to avoid it, in any form, at any time. Or because we're smart, strong women, we think we won't fall prey to anything. Or we think if we hang on a little bit longer, a miracle will occur. Maybe we'll claw our way back to our damn skis (and you KNOW how unrealistic THAT line of thinking is, especially when you consider how easy it is to claw water). It's almost like we are in disbelief that the cycle has come back around again. And again. And again.

So, we hang on and hang on and hang on until . . . we don't. Either we let go, or something FORCES us to let go. BAM. WIPEOUT. Cool beans.

How do we know when it's the right time to let go? How do we make that happen? Is there a super-secret trick? Or are we doomed to keep glubbing along until the driver kills the boat motor and puts us out of our misery?

Let's discuss.

BFF,
Lisa and Carleen

P.S. Have you ever stopped to consider the brilliance of the word, "derp"? Really . . . just take a moment and think about it. It's Batman language, like POW! and WHAMMO! and SLUG!

Chapter Twelve

LISA STORIES

Mind the Gap!

I've known Doug since the seventh grade. Once we graduated from high school in 1988, many people in our class lost touch for a long time. Especially those of us who moved away. Fortunately, I discovered Facebook as a viable option for communication at our twenty-year reunion. I was resistant at first (because seriously, this is what my kids at school were doing, so, ummmm . . . no), but it's where I reconnected with Doug and many other classmates.

I will admit that I've been reading Doug's spiritual posts on Facebook for two years and I rarely understand what he's saying. This is fascinating to me because I consider myself to be a fairly intelligent adult. Having said that, he posted something in the spring of 2018 that not only did I understand, but it almost made my head explode.

"A defined identity becomes so strong that it eventually creates a paradisiacal situation, but that strength binds us to that place when we would transform further. There has to come about a wide gap between what had been our paradise, and what we now experience, if we are to transform beyond yesterday. Suffering descrambles former programming, opening us up to new revelation, and these new thoughts have children, the new selves we become."
—Doug Wentz

Now, I'm not 100 percent sure how Doug meant it, but I know how I took it. Now, A.) I am not a fan of suffering, but B.) I had been hanging out in the gap for a DAMN long time. I didn't let go until recently, and I wasn't even aware of how hard I was clinging to the past. I put up a huge stink for years and fought to exhaustion. I was desperately searching for normal (whatever

the hell THAT is).

I was holding on so tightly to what I thought was my identity and to my idea of what paradise was that my present barely had a chance. I have been stuck in the gap for an awfully long time. Decades. Different people, different times, different things, different reasons. I am stubborn and horribly bullheaded. When I make my mind up about something, it is hard to change it. And I was confident that someday my normal would come back. And please, don't get me wrong. I have had a lot of happiness so far in my adult life, and I have made excellent memories with many amazing humans, but in the back of my mind I was still always searching. And waiting.

How many years did I spend with unrealistic expectations? Let's not do the math, mmmmk?

I wasn't necessarily living IN the past, but I was definitely pining FOR the past. I was living for that time in my life where things were awesome. I had no idea things would never be that way again. Things . . . would . . . never . . . be that way again. And I wasn't willing to accept many new normals unless they conformed with my idea of happiness. It didn't occur to me to let go of the past (at least a little, for Pete's sake!) and fully create and attend to my present. You can certainly carry elements of the past into your present, but sheesh! In the corners of my mind where I was holding out this hope, I was totally doin' it wrong.

So, when things kept going wrong for me, I was profoundly affected. My heart shattered. Every time. Until very recently, it never occurred to me that my idea of paradise was inaccessible. You can't recreate your past. You can only move forward . . . or hang out in the gap. Once I figured out what I'd been doing (two months ago, but whatever . . .), I just needed to redefine paradise. So that's where I am at. Picking up the pieces of my blown mind.

We all write our own stories with every decision we make. We are not powerless in this life. Take that pain and let it fuel your new life. Let go of the past, stay out of the gap, and start creating your #EXTRA!

Well, That Didn't Go as Planned: Part 2

Isn't it adorable how you have preconceived notions of how your child is going to be? I mean, it's cute how you have no idea what could be coming at you at full speed. You have no idea which Wile E. Coyote wake-up call will bless you right upside the head. (Did you know the E. stands for Ethelbert? Me, either.) Which way is it coming from? BOOM! You don't GET to

know! You need to be prepared for things that are impossible to prepare for. And sometimes you not only have to let go of the rope, but you may need to let your child take the lead . . . I know, right?

The next generation—guitar version! (#Lili)

I look at my Great-Grandpa Walter Appel, who walked 1,000 miles out of Germany to Russia at age nineteen. He had nothing but the shirt on his back when he boarded a boat bound for America, where he knew exactly nobody. That is pretty fierce, right? You want to know what else is fierce? Parenting an LGBTQIA teen. Even today, in 2018. So, I dunno, Grandpa, it might be a tossup! Kidding not kidding.

With ALL. OF. MY. EXPERIENCE in this area, I was not as prepared as I would have fancied myself. Granted, there were some twists, but OH EM GEEZY! I had to let go of the rope AND the wheel. I had no choice if I wanted any sort of positive outcome for my baby, my sweet one, my only child.

If ever there's a time in school that's crappy, people pretty universally agree it's junior high, right? You look the worst you have ever looked, you are growing (sometimes painfully), you are starting to break out, and hair is growing in places you just don't want it. You are starting to notice members of the opposite OR the same sex, and it is all very awkward, at best. The hormones can be as bad for boys as it is for girls. And there is drama. So, you're going to try to date someone feeling and looking as awkward as possible. It is a total recipe for success, right? Yeah. Take this and add ANY sort of difference and even under the best of circumstances, things can get brutal.

If it was just that Kiddo were gay? No big deal. When she first told me, I was like, yeah, okay! In fact, I kind of did a happy dance because her potential incidence of #MeToo dropped. A lot. But our journey was a little different, and it is still evolving. Kris, my husband, and I were dealing with things we had never dealt with before and learning terms we were unfamiliar with. There are so many. Thankfully, Kiddo was very patient with us. And at this point, I need to give a huge shout-out to Laura and Ashley. I love you both. You saved us. Without you, I would be in a very different place right now and I would not have the wherewithal to write a book.

Fall of Kiddo's eighth grade year was when our world blew up. Llamicles were flying EVERY-

WHERE and it took the rest of the year to herd them back into the corral. This is all fairly recent, but I'm happy to say it is solidly in the past, and I do have Kiddo's permission to talk about this.

Elementary school was pretty good! She went to a Spanish Immersion school in the area. She had a great education and great teachers. She formed good friendships and good relationships with the teachers and the staff. I have nothing but good things to say about that experience.

The summer between sixth and seventh grade was amazing! We were presented with an opportunity for Kiddo to spend five weeks in Spain with a lovely family, who would then turn around and send their daughter to stay with us for eight weeks. So Aranxta, her host mother, and I planned and planned for months until the day arrived to start this adventure! And, of course, Kris and I brought her to Spain, because OF COURSE we did because #SPAIN! When Carlota came back with Kiddo right before school started, we had two daughters for eight weeks! It was a wonderful experience! But almost right after Carlota went home, things started to unravel. Kiddo got slammed with the Huge Evil Anvil of Hormone Hell and was also dealing with the Gender Identity Beastie.

Toward the end of seventh grade, Kiddo decided to lop off her long, beautiful, Spanish sun-streaked, strawberry-blonde hair. Fine. Shortly thereafter, she came out as gay. Fine. Toward the end of the school year, she wanted to start wearing boy's clothing. Fine. We tried to do Swedish Camp at Concordia Language Villages that summer. She had attended the summer prior to Spain and loved it! But the Anxiety Beastie was too powerful, and we had to come pick her up after the first night. One day of camp. $2,000. Holy SH*T, but fine. I let her get her nose pierced. It's little and cute like mine. So, whatever, fine. Then she wanted to shave around her head, leave hair on top and color it red. Jessica-Rabbit red. Then teal. Cringed a little, but fine. Then she wanted a name change at school. A male name. All these things were very important to her sense of self at the time. And, of course we talked this stuff through. All of it. Sometimes for months on end.

My twenty-six years of teaching experience didn't prepare me for what I would really do in this situation. You cannot say what you'd do until you look into the eyes of your child. And then you choose your reaction and your words very carefully because YOU mean the world to your kid. A lot depends on you. This is why I say that not only do you have to let go at times, but sometimes you need to let your child lead. As a sidebar, Kiddo now thinks the Hair Fiasco was one of the worst decisions she has ever made. But she needed the freedom to make that decision and learn from it. Even our hairdresser, whom I adore, said, "Mom, it's only hair. It

grows back. It can be colored. Let her experiment with her hair so she doesn't go experiment with other things." Ralph speaks the truth!

I think if Kiddo had waited until senior high to bust out all of this stuff, it would have been a different ball of wax. Her classmates in junior high were not equipped to gracefully deal with her. She had a team that stuck up for her, but her team wasn't with her 24/7. And the adults in the building, who did everything possible to keep my kid comfortable, accepted, and safe, could not monitor other kids 24/7. When the bullying started, my kid came at the offenders with double middle fingers blazing, and baby llama hooves up. That is my kid, but this was not helpful. Understandable, but not helpful. When a major self-harm event happened, we had to take action. It was at that point we moved Kiddo to a smaller, special school that helps kids deal with big emotions. We didn't realize it at the time, but it was a huge blessing.

We met with the new school people on the Wednesday before Thanksgiving and Kiddo started that next Monday. The first month or two were bumpy, but now that she's done with the program completion, she said she loved the experience and that everybody should have to go through a program like that for the social, emotional component. Kiddo now has better coping skills than many adults. I am super proud of all she has accomplished and yet I am also sad. I am sad my child has dealt with deeper and tougher things in the past fourteen years than I ever had to.

So, the mental health piece. Tied directly to the gender identity piece. Tied directly to other people and how they respond. And then back again. Here we go 'round the mulberry bush. It is hard enough to have people all up in your grill and questioning you as an adult. Can you imagine having to do it as a child? Sadly, many of you probably can imagine. Maybe you have been there. Maybe someone you love has been there. Maybe someone you love IS there. Maybe you are there. Well, if you haven't gotten the drift yet, this is a very safe place for ALL people. Period. We don't play. And I DO give hard llama kicks.

Just Show Up

Seriously, though, just show up for life. Sometimes you HAVE to let go in order to do this. If you are taking facefuls of water and you're gasping for air . . . LET GO OF THE ROPE. You can't show up if you're underwater. You have nothing to prove, but you ARE depriving yourself of oxygen. Don't let your preconceived notion of how life should be get in the way of you living your true life. You can't control everything. You can't control most things. So, control what you can—typically that's limited to you, yourself, and you. How will YOU react? Whatcha gonna do?

My mom was pretty indispensable teaching me how to show up. Every time I threw a huge fit about how I was SO done (believe me, there were some loud hella doozy hissy fits), done with it all of it because eff EVERYTHING. I had completely had it with men. But Mom would always say, "Keep an open heart." I didn't know then that I would never get my paradise back, but my mom knew if I closed my heart, then I would remain in the gap between pain and growth and would never move forward.

"Life will break you. Nobody can protect you from that, and living alone won't either, for solitude will also break you with its yearning. You have to love. You have to feel. It is the reason you are here on earth. You are here to risk your heart. You are here to be swallowed up. And when it happens that you are broken, or betrayed, or left, or hurt, or death brushes near, let yourself sit by an apple tree and listen to the apples falling all around you in heaps, wasting their sweetness. Tell yourself you tasted as many as you could." —Louise Erdrich, The Painted Drum

Thank you, Louise, for validating my entire adult life.

The Dog Ate My Chair

#DogsTeetheToo (#Lili)

I have a little patio table and chair set. It is wooden and painted a milky blue. It was the first piece of furniture I bought after I moved out of my house in Minneapolis. It was the move that happened after the dissolution of my second marriage. I felt sad and unsure of everything, but I so loved this little table and chairs! Mom and Dad were shopping with me, and I asked their opinion. Even though money was extremely tight, I bought it and Mom and Dad helped me carry it out. It was perfect!

That table and chairs have lived in one apartment, one rented condo, one purchased condo, and finally our current home. They resided on the patio outside our front door. Fast forward four years, and there's a new puppy in the family. We named her Lucy, but we mostly call her Goose! She brings us so much joy, and even Buddy, her older brother, now loves her. (Buddy was really mad for a couple of months after she came to live with us.)

I have never had a pet in my adult life that chews on things. Until Lucy. She was a present for Kiddo's combined golden birthday/Christmas present. Lucy was spendy. And she was super stealthy about her chewing activity. I came out to the patio one day and one corner on one

of the chairs was completely gnawed! After the second corner had been gnawed, I noticed a teeny tiny doggo tooth on the deck next to the chair. I realized our Goosey Girl was teething and using my chair as a teething ring!

On the one hand it was super cute, but on the other it made me feel emotionally constipated. I thought about why it was upsetting to me. When I left our house in Minneapolis, I had to leave some things behind. I couldn't take everything I wanted to take as I was moving from a house to a one-bedroom apartment. There were a couple of pieces of furniture that made my heart hurt when I closed the front door for the last time. That added to the significance of my little table and chair set. It represented the beginning of my new life!

I could have fixed it, but I didn't. I think I need to leave it as is. My old way of thinking was, "I need to either fix or replace this because when this marriage falls apart, I will need a table and chairs for my new place." Uff da, right? Ashley, best therapist in the universe, once said, "This is not PTSD, but a series of small traumas that can feel like a big trauma." Although she was not talking about my table and chairs incident, or even talking about me, it really made me think. It has been no small task to rid myself of that knee-jerk stress response. The one where no relationship in your life will work out because none of them have so far, and you are in your (late) forties. History has taught me all relationships are temporary. Intellectually, I knew this thinking was flawed, but try telling that to my heart! For a long time, my heart wasn't having that business. At all.

So, two things: I needed to let go of that thinking, and I needed to let go of my table and chairs. And I did. I let them go.

Chapter Thirteen

CARLEEN STORIES

The Sweats, Public Humiliation, and Me: The Early Years

This is the story of a time when I got a MAJOR face full of water. Playing the flute. In a big, blue Cinderella dress. In front of pretty much my whole town.

Before I get to that part of the story, let me give you a little bit of background to set the stage. (See what I did there?)

My brother Kevin (who I had always thought was the coolest person ever) brought home a drum set one summer from the local community college that he attended. "Jack and Diane" was in heavy rotation in our house at the time, and Kevin wanted to learn how to play that iconic drum solo. Because he did it, I wanted to do it too. So, when he was at work for the day, I sat where he sat, I turned on the tape deck like he did, and I banged away at the drums and cymbals like there was no tomorrow.

I was convinced it was my destiny to be a drummer.

When the time came to test for band in fourth grade, I did not hesitate for one second before circling "percussion" on the form that asked which instrument I was interested in. I could hardly breathe as the pride swelled in my chest. My brother would see I was following in his footsteps—his little shadow, his faithful, worshipful protégé. I could almost hear him clap for me as I scraped my pencil on that half sheet of paper. I knew he was going to be so proud. Plus, I had an in with the Big Wig: the director who came to administer the test happened to be Mr. Frandsen, Kevin and Cissy's choir director and an absolute LEGEND of a teacher in

town. I figured he had the same sea-parting power as Moses, and because he liked my siblings, I knew my music test was a simple formality. I was IN. I was going to rock. Maybe even play a solo. On a drum set.

I was disappointed weeks later when I saw I had been assigned to play the flute.

The flute? What? That didn't make ANY sense. SURELY my music test had proven I was going to be the best drummer Virginia Public Schools—maybe even the WORLD—had ever seen. Flute? Seriously? There must have been some mistake. I was born to rock. I was born to be like Kevin. I believed that so deeply, I mustered up every ounce of shy-girl bravery I had and approached Mr. Frandsen.

After a brief discussion, I sat back down. Huh. Somehow, the results of my music test had gotten lost. Mr. Frandsen had put me in the flute section, and there I would stay. I hung my head, but because I was a good girl, I obeyed.

My mom went to Schmitt Music on Chestnut Street and signed the paperwork to rent a basic Armstrong flute in a blue velvet-lined case. There would be no big drum solo for this girl.

But as usual, I got used to the idea.

When my other brother Cedric heard me toot out my first few notes, he was over the moon. Pretty soon, he told me I should go to Paris to study with Jean-Pierre Rampal. Now, if you don't know who that is, no worries. When I first heard that name, I didn't know, either. But if Big Brother (like what Sally calls Charlie Brown, not the ominous entity in *1984*) said he was a big deal, then I believed him. And if Cedric—who I adored, even if he wasn't as cool as Kevin—said I should do something with that certain sparkle in his eye, then I figured I'd better get busy figuring out how to do it.

Cedric was a classical music lover. When I say "lover," I mean LOVE-ER. He spent many Friday nights hanging out with Beethoven and Haydn and Mozart. He knew the names of #AllTheSymphoniesAndMovements. He would have totally been able to Name That (Classical) Tune with one note, thank you very much. And if anyone showed the least bit of interest in his music, he was all over it.

Now, I didn't love classical music the way I loved Kevin's rock and roll, but I liked it well enough. And I was the good girl who listened to her teacher in class and practiced faithfully in the House with Paper-Thin Walls. And Cedric's dream of his little sister going to Paris grew

with every passing year.

That is, until he died.

I was fifteen years old and quietly distraught over the loss of Big Brother.

Practicing my flute became really, really painful. Cedric was no longer there to hear me and talk to me about my future while his eyes sparkled. He didn't talk to me about anything at all. He was just . . . gone. And my heart was broken.

Even though it lost some of its appeal, I kept playing. And I had enough talent to do pretty well without a lot of practice. Cedric's Paris dream was replaced by one of my own: I was going to be a Flute Goddess, just like Paula and Lynn, two high school girls who had occupied the first-chair position in the high school band. (If you aren't a band person, all you need to know is the first chair player is the best in the section.)

Being a Flute Goddess meant you would be chosen—no, anointed—not only to play the piccolo (the cutest instrument), but also to wear a pretty formal dress to your senior concert, float to the front of the stage, and play a solo in front of your friends, family, the whole town, and God—accompanied by the WHOLE BAND. All Flute Goddesses played the same song: "Some Concerto in Something Major No. Something" by Somebody Important. I don't remember what it was called. I can hear the beginning of it in my head, so if I hear it on the elevator or somewhere else, I immediately recognize it before breaking out in The Sweats.

I remember the exact moment Mr. Vukmanich (my band director, my best guy friend's dad, and another Teacher Legend in our town) held up the sheet music during my private lesson. It was the Holy Grail, the Shroud of Turin, and Excalibur all rolled into one. His facial expression seemed to say, "Are you ready for this? I think you are."

I looked at all the black on the page and thought, Um, maybe . . . ? but my smile screamed, "YES!" The song looked terribly difficult—the hardest piece I had ever attempted. I had absolutely NO idea how I was going to pull it off. But I thought, Hey, things usually work out. I usually find my way. Right? Right.

WRONG.

I knew the exact next moment I wasn't going to be able to do it. Like—the exact next microsecond. There was a still, small voice in my head that said, Carleen . . . you're a darling. Really.

And you're a pretty decent flute player. First chair, even. But you're not really a Flute Goddess. "Some Concerto in Something Major No. Something" by Somebody Important is just not in your wheelhouse. Hand it back to him.

But I didn't. I took that sheet music, and I began playing it right there in Mr. V.'s office. It didn't go that badly, really, and I liked the way the music sounded. With every note I was able to play, the possibility I could really become the next Paula or Lynn became clearer and clearer, and I walked out of Malone Hall standing a little taller and smiling a little broader.

Now, picture a female version of Kevin Arnold from *The Wonder Years*: that was me. A well-meaning, nice, and earnest kid with entirely too much optimism for her own good. A well-meaning, nice, earnest, and overly optimistic kid you just knew was going to turn into a train wreck, and there wasn't a damn thing you could do about it except watch the carnage unfold.

I'm not going to completely drag this out, so let me summarize the two to three months leading up to our senior-year spring band concert and let's see if you start developing The Sweats too.

- I practiced . . . but I had no clue what I was doing. Like, at all. There was no YouTube filled with all the how-to tutorials that exist nowadays. We couldn't afford private lessons. Money was so tight, we wouldn't have been able to afford free lessons.

- I started from the beginning every time I dragged myself, kicking and screaming, into my bedroom to practice. When it got hard, I quit for the night . . . and then I shoved the song in the back of my band folder. (Smooth, Carleen. Real smooth.)

- Every time I picked up my flute to play, I thought about Cedric. My heart instantly sagged, every time. I missed him. I ached for him. And I just didn't have the same musical spark in me anymore. Playing alone—without the ability to fold myself into the whole band—made me hurt too much because me doing so was what Cedric had wanted. But I just kept going because that's what Good Girls like me do. Wait—let me correct that: I kept going, and I didn't voice my pain out loud. Because that's what Good Girls do.

- My overly busy director didn't have time to work with me on "Some Concerto in Something Major No. Something" by Somebody Important. He had too many moving parts making up his position as the director of a powerhouse band program in a small town to be able to work with me as often as I would have needed him to. And he probably

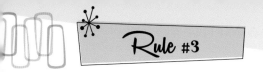

believed I would come through enough to pull off a semi-decent performance . . . somehow. As a teacher myself, I totally understand this—you just can't do #AllTheThings—or you might not even realize that #AllThoseThingsOverThere need doing. There are just a whole lot of spinning plates all around you.

The day of the performance arrived. We had our dress rehearsal during fourth hour, and "Some Concerto in Something Major No. Something" by Somebody Important did not go well. At all. I knew that I was a "nerves" kind of girl, so I brushed it off.

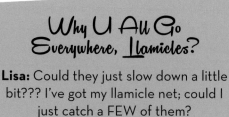

Why U All Go Everywhere, Llamicles?

Lisa: Could they just slow down a little bit??? I've got my llamicle net; could I just catch a FEW of them?

Me trying to keep all of my #Llamicles together! Does it look like I'm succeeding? (#Lili)

Seventh hour of Performance Day arrived. There was a knock at the door of my classroom, and when I looked up, there was Mr. V. He looked right at me, pointed, and motioned me outside. I got up and met him in the hallway, and he closed the door behind me. He was holding the program for the night's performance, and he opened it up to show me where my Flute Goddess solo was in the lineup. And then he said something that no teacher—no adult—no human—had ever said to me.

"Carleen, I want to let you know you don't have to play your solo tonight if you aren't ready. We can just pass right over it—see? We can move from this song to that song, and we don't need to say anything to the audience about it. We'll just skip it. We didn't really have time to rehearse it enough. What do you think?"

I was horrified. Me? Not play "Some Concerto in Something Major No. Something" by Somebody Important? NO WAY! I was first chair! I was following in the footsteps of Paula! And Lynn! I had a gorgeous turquoise-blue Cinderella dress that had a hoop skirt and puffy shoulders and a BUTT BOW. I had my grandmother's double-strand pearls to wear. I had an obnoxiously sparkly hair clip to nestle in my freshly hairsprayed perm. I had big sparkly earrings. I had WHITE SHOES WITH SILVER INLAY TEARDROPS FROM PAYLESS SHOE SOURCE TO WEAR, JUST LIKE A CINDERELLA FLUTE GODDESS SHOULD.

"Thanks, Mr. V., but I'm going to play. I'll be all right."

"Are you sure? Because we can totally skip it and keep going."

"I'm sure. Thanks, though."

People. The Universe had totally handed me an out. I would be willing to bet Cedric was talking into Mr. V.'s ear that morning, saying, "Don't let her do it. Talk her out of it. C'mon, man! Do.not.let.her.humiliate.herself.in.front.of.EVERYBODY."

Bestie Kerri and I posing before senior prom. I wish I had kept the Cinderella dress and all the accompanying accouterments. (#Lini)

The evening of the performance arrived—my very last band concert in Virginia High School's Goodman Auditorium. I was in my Cinderella dress and shoes. My hair was especially puffy. I had my grandmother's pearls on. My obnoxious hair clip sparkled. My friends and I posed for pictures together in our gymnasium holding tank one last time. One last time.

How many songs did we play before it was time for "Some Concerto in Something Major No. Something" by Somebody Important? Two? Three? It doesn't matter. All that mattered was my moment in the spotlight was coming, ready or not.

I. Was. Not. Ready. In fact, do you want to know the real truth? I don't think I had played the whole song through once with the band. Come to think of it, I don't think I had played the whole song through once BY MYSELF. Ever.

I imagine Mr. V. had The Sweats as I stood up and adjusted my stand and sheet music. But to his credit, he raised his baton. The band raised their instruments, and off we went.

I'm going to spare you the details. Actually, I'm going to spare MYSELF the details.

Just picture the worst possible performance. Ever. Then dial it up another fifteen notches. And then fifteen more.

Band musicians, my mouth was a dry as when you wake up after sleeping with it open for two hours. I had that "layer of paste" thing going on. We didn't have disposable bottles of water at

that time, but it wouldn't have mattered if I had a gallon jug sitting near my music stand. There would be no moisture in my mouth that night. It was all coming out of my pores.

The Sweats.

I went down as the Anti-Flute Goddess that night. I think there might be a plaque somewhere in a janitor's closet on the third floor with my name engraved on a single, lonely strip of tarnished brass. Carleen Saima Matts—Anti-Flute Goddess. The One and Only, forevermore.

Was I trying to please my brother, my other brother, my band director, my other band director, myself, my bus driver, or someone else? Was it my pride? Was it my fear of admitting I couldn't do something? Was it shame I was failing at something, and someone I respected noticed and called me on it? Was I frozen, thinking everyone would notice me sitting there—the big, fat failure? Was it all these things?

Probably.

I could have stopped. I could have sat down, walked off the stage, or stood there and let the band play the rest of the song. But I didn't . . . I kept going. And . . . I'm sure it was a sight to see. Everyone loves a train wreck . . . and I'm sure I gave the gossip mill a TON of material that night.

And . . . that's all I have to say about that.

Except this one thing: I'm sorry, Mr. V. I'm really, truly sorry to have put you through that. I know you knew I was going to crash and burn, but you let me do it, anyway. It took me a long time to learn my lesson about letting go of the rope because I have crashed and burned a few times since then . . . but you had the honor of witnessing the very first time.

Aging and Alzheimer's

Nancy tells me not to sweat this aging thing. "It's natural. It's what the human body was designed to do. We're born, we live our lives, we age, and we die. We can delay it a while with hormones and clean eating and exercise, but eventually it catches up to all of us . . . and it's not a bad thing at all. It's life."

I like Nancy, my physician's assistant (read: Hormone Guru). She's older than I am, wise, and

self-confident in a way I someday hope to be. She is the one medical professional who really listened to me as I described what my perimenopausal body was up to now that I'd lost my uterus to a prolapse and the resulting hysterectomy. She helped me understand that no, my ovaries weren't going about their normal business just because they still floated around in the same vicinity they had before their feisty neighbor mysteriously disappeared one December morning. (Things were very, very different in Carleenietown after that.)

Yes, Nancy is great. I can talk to her about anything. She listens to me, and she gets me. That's why I hate what she has to say about aging. I know she's right, but I don't want her to be.

Like many women, I could do without aging. I hate seeing new racing stripes in my hair. I hate the wrinkles around my eyes. I hate how the skin on my shoulders looks when I raise my arms above my head (even though I know I earned that skin during many hours in the sun). I hate the way my body puckers and sighs in its losing battle with gravity. I hate that even looking sideways at something sweet makes me gain five pounds, usually in the worst places. And I hate seeing evidence all around me that the older I get, the less society values me.

> ## Beware the Battle Eyebrows
>
> **Lisa:** Lisa: I have Battle Eyebrows. If I come at you with them, you better pray you can run faster than I do. My brows have superpowers! #RunFasterThanMyEyebrows

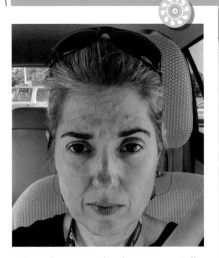

My eyebrows speak volumes, especially when I'm in angry Mama Llama mode! (#Lili)

I can't work out as hard as I used to before my surgery, and I don't have money for the mommy body lifts, Botox treatments, and spider vein removal that I'm not supposed to want. I don't want to pay for lasers (yet) to remove those unsightly age spots on my face that don't give a rat's behind about the potions I've used to try to lighten and brighten them. And if I did have money for all that, I'd probably come out looking like Frankenstein's awkward cousin who tried too hard—you know, the vain one who can't make a natural expression anymore.

So, I do my best to not let it bother me too much. It's a process that involves me avoiding mirrors and wearing loose clothing to disguise the extra ten-plus pounds I carry around now

that I am short a uterus. I know my husband loves me just the way I am, and no one notices or cares about all that stuff as much as I do (unless that person is trying to sell me a product or a service). I know that what I look like on the outside has no bearing on who I am on the inside.

But I've been thinking, and something has dawned on me.

The worry over and despising of the aging process is really just a cover up for something nestled deeper in my psyche: I'm scared to death of losing my mom. And because of Alzheimer's, I'm losing beloved parts of her much too soon—parts that I carry in my memories because they are gone from hers.

This is one of my favorite pictures with my mama. She had this incredible laugh that you could only see, not hear (at first). She loved the lake so much. (#Lini)

When I go to visit her, I see a sweet, little lady who looks exactly like my mom. This woman laughs all the time, especially when she sees "that old lady" in pictures of her. She is social and well-liked at the memory care facility where she lives because she is adorable. The little white-haired men sitting at the tables near the door tell her to behave herself when she leaves with me, and without missing a beat, she tells them to do the same. All of this is wonderful. She is healthy, happy, and loved by everyone who knows her. But she is a different version of herself now, and absolutely none of the changes I see in her are her fault.

There are certain things only your mother knows about you: how it felt to have you in her pregnant belly and how it felt to look at your face for the first time; what the rocking chair sounded like in the middle of the night when she soothed you back to sleep after a bad dream; how fun it was to eat a McDonald's fish sandwich and tease sixteen-year-old you about the cute boy at the next table.

And there are things about you a few people know, but it feels best when your mom remembers them: what it was like buying a pretty dress, baking Christmas cookies, celebrating your birthday, and holding the newborn you waited much too long for.

And there are moments when you know you annoyed your mother: when you hiccuped and giggled through her mother's funeral, when you didn't help with cleaning enough, when you didn't want to tear yourself away from the television to visit your ailing grandfather, and when you almost burned the house down by turning the sauna stove to high instead of off.

And there are moments you've shared with your mom that you know shaped your character, even though you had to struggle through them: the suicide of your big brother, the chronic yelling and subsequent silent treatment at the family dinner table, the sudden death of your father just when you started to figure out your relationship with him, the loss of your childhood home, and the pain of divorce.

My mother has lost most, if not all, of those memories. For the time being, she knows who I am when she sees me, she recognizes her cute and helpful grandson, and she knows that when we come to visit her, she is in for small adventures that bring her joy in the moment. Before we left her recently, Matthew put his hands on her shoulders and said, "We'll see you in a month for Christmas, Grandma." She looked him in the eyes and said very sincerely, "Don't forget."

I want her to remember. I want her to remember taking me to our friend Lorraine's place to have alterations done on my strapless prom dresses and giggling when Lorraine asked me if I was sure I didn't want her to add a turtleneck. I want her to remember the road trip she and I took together in the big brown van to Hot Springs, South Dakota, to help my sister after the birth of her first child, Amy. I want her to remember how she used to buy Me the Awkward Teenager a few new items of clothing, even though we couldn't really afford it (and knowing we would have to combine all the bags into one before we got home so Dad wouldn't yell at us for spending too much of his money).

I want her to remember making her special chocolate chip cookies and pancakes and apple pie, stroking my forehead with her rough hands when I was heartbroken over a boy, and telling me she loved to hear me practice my flute, even when I couldn't get the hang of my senior solo piece to save my life. I want her to remember taking walks with Dad during the last few years of his life, picking up nice pieces of quartz from the gravel of Poirier Road. I want her to remember bringing a mason jar of quartz rocks to his grave.

I want her to remember that day in the car on the way home from Lake Vermilion when my seven- or eight-year-old self first grasped the concept of mortality. I started weeping and told her I didn't want her to die. She quieted my despair that day by saying to me, "Carleen, we're all going to die. My parents are both gone, and someday I will be gone too, but it won't happen for a long, long time. And then I'll be in heaven, so I'll be all right, and so will you. And you will be someone's mom by then, and you will be taking care of your own kids."

That was fewer than forty years ago. The time she spoke of is just around the corner, and I don't like it one bit.

Rule #3

Waterskiing Women of a Certain Season

Being a WWCS is all about having grit, resiliency, and ganas! It is what the Finns call "Sisu": the force that makes you stand up an eighth time after falling down seven times.

THIS is what makes us persist! It is all about accepting that what you need is what you need.

We must listen to our inner voice. We must say, I am worth standing up for! And if I am the only one standing, so be it! I am enough! And by standing up together, we make the world a better place. This is not about ego; it is about owning our greatness and using it for good. Don't pretend to be perfect—own your powerful imperfection and move forward!

A lunch date with publisher #AmyGato and editor #RhiaPusheen at The Bad Waitress in Minneapolis. #GOTeamEXTRA!

Maybe it's because I am the youngest and an "oops," and forty-five-ish seems much too young to become an orphan. Maybe it's because forty years from now, which doesn't seem like a long, long time at all, my son may be in the same position as I am, wondering what has become of the woman who made those special cookies for him and his friends, sang at the top of her lungs with him during mother-son road trips, told him how much she liked hearing him play his trumpet, and cheered him on at almost every single sports game. Maybe it's because I don't want to lose my beloved sister a piece at a time, the way my mom lost hers. Maybe it's because I don't want to be the woman sleeping in the reclining chair in front of the TV in the memory care unit, with her husband sitting next to her with his hand on her heart and his head resting gently next to hers.

It hurts to have those feelings, and I know the men in my life don't want me to fall apart when I lose my mom. So, I write, and I cry sometimes when I am alone with my feelings. And sometimes I cry around them, and they talk to me and help me see my way through my emotions and recognize that my mom isn't hurting through this experience. She is doing quite well, and she has earned this peaceful time after a lifetime of hardship. I take a deep breath and reach down inside myself for some sisu—that Finnish strength that makes you stand up an eighth time after falling for a seventh—the strength my mother has modeled for me my entire life.

When I can get back home to the Iron Range, I break my mom out of the memory care facility, taking her out to the lake to sit by the beach for a few minutes, or on a quick run to Ben Franklin, or out for a meal so she can have her beloved fish, knowing full well she will order a hamburger instead.

During those times, I am her mother, and I hold it together. I hold her hand and buckle her seat belt. And when I say goodbye, I give her two extra kisses and three extra hugs, telling her I love her and will see her again really soon—over and over so she won't forget. At least when I leave her, I see she has people around her who notice her, talk with her, give her food to eat, and keep her safe. She isn't alone in her too-quiet apartment anymore. That makes it easier to get in the car and get back to my busy life, but I still miss her deeply and wish I were there to see her every day.

I suppose I complain about my greying hair and wrinkling face because that is my way of saying I don't want my mom to die, even though I know she will. I also know as I write, I should be getting to some big revelation about seizing the day and not taking people and my health for granted, but the truth is that I am still that little girl who sat in the car with her mom and believed she had lots of time.

I can feel the day is getting closer when she will not know our faces anymore when she sees us. I know that because of this disease, her personality might drastically change, and she might need to sleep most of the time. I know eventually her brain will forget how to keep her alive. With Alzheimer's, you lose your loved ones multiple times before the last time, and the whole process makes me so sad.

I survived losing my dad, even though it still hurts sometimes, and I will survive losing my mom too, when the time comes. I have no doubt she will be just fine, as she said, and I know from experience that the sisu my parents instilled in me will get me through the toughest times. And maybe it's good she has lost the painful memories that kept her from laughing as much as she does now. When you experience her laughter, it's like seeing her distilled down to her finest essence. When I lament that Alzheimer's might take over my brain someday, Matthew reassures me that scientists will discover a cure by then, so I shouldn't worry. I hope he's right, so he and Scott don't have to go through this long goodbye. But if they do, I hope my finest essence is as beautiful as my mother's.

We lost Mama in 2017. My nieces remembered her in 2018 with clippings from her lilies and wildflowers from the road by her old house. They and their brothers brought a similar bouquet for her casket. (#Lini)

In the end, Nancy's and my mom's words are true: we are all going to die, for it's what we were made to do. Coming to terms with it all is a whole other story that I am still writing.

Joann Louise Waltanen Matts
August 30, 1931–July 15, 2017
Rest in Peace, Cute Mom

Chapter Fourteen

YOUR TURN!

Take some time to write about Letting Go in your life. You might want to use some of the prompts below or go your own direction. Do what feels natural and right for you and listen to what your writing tells you about yourself and your life.

- Tell about a time when you wiped out—but you hung on to the rope and got a faceful of water. What was that like? Why do you think you did that?
- Tell about a time when you wiped out—but you let go of the rope. What was that like? Why do you think you did that?
- What patterns do you notice about times when you hung on and times when you let go?
- Does letting go feel like a victory or a failure? Why?
- Who are the people who stand with you and help you? What do they do for you?
- When have you positively helped others? Or, when could you positively help others in the future? What was that like/what could that be like for you?
- My biggest "a-ha" related to this section is . . . because . . .
- I hope to . . .
- I am grateful for . . .

Chapter Fifteen

#SPINGOLD: RELEASE YOUR GRIP

Idea #1: Put Down Your Damn Suitcases!

Back in chapter 10, we talked about the concept of forgiveness and how Oprah taught us it's all about giving up the hope that the past can be anything different than what it is. We also discussed that even when YOU are the one who did the hurting, it is mucho importante that you forgive yourself because you are an imperfect human being who makes mistakes, often because you have experienced hurt yourself. And if you forgive yourself and move forward, you have the ability to make the world better because you are using your sh*t as fertilizer for something else more beautiful.

That's all nice and everything, right? It's probably even possible to do that for, like, five minutes. But what happens when IT. KEEPS. COMING. BACK, no matter what you do?

Ah, yes. That.

There are a couple of things we need to talk about, and we're going to bring in another Soul Sister to help us out. If you don't know Brené Brown yet, you absolutely must spend some time with her, either by listening to her speak on YouTube (she's done a ton of public speaking, including a TED Talk) or by reading some of her books, which are, in a word, amazeballs.

Our favorite book of hers is *The Gifts of Imperfection*, and it is the kind of book you will want to read more than once AND gift to everyone you know. In it, she describes her work as a shame researcher and what she learned about love, belonging, vulnerability, and the freeing power of owning one's story.

If we could reprint the whole book here, we would. Seriously. Go buy it, borrow it from a friend, or get it from the library. She says everything with such beauty and grace and goodness—so much so, you will want to ugly-cry. It's pure magic. SHE is pure magic. Just like you. :)

One of our biggest takeaways from her work when it comes to self-forgiveness is that there is a difference between GUILT and SHAME. If you feel guilt, you feel that you DID something bad. (Totally appropriate.) If you feel shame, however, you feel that you ARE bad. (Totally destructive!)

Whew. Go back and read that last part one more time. Do you see how powerful that is? Now, what if you are living in shame ALL THE TIME? What if all you tell yourself, day in and day out, is that YOU are bad? What can you do about it?

Brown writes,

> Shame needs three things to grow out of control in our lives: secrecy, silence, and judgment. When something shaming happens and we keep it locked up, it festers and grows. It consumes us. We need to share our experience. Shame happens between people, and it heals between people. If we can find someone who has earned the right to hear our story, we need to tell it. Shame loses power when it is spoken . . .

> Shame is about fear, blame, and disconnection. Story is about worthiness and embracing the imperfections that bring us courage, compassion, and connection. If we want to live fully, without the constant fear of not being enough, we have to own our story. (*The Gifts of Imperfection*)

I (Carleen) have been in this place a few times in my life—one period in particular I like to call the Twilight Zone. I'm not going to get into detail about what happened then (because remember, Sister Brené also tells us that "not everyone deserves to know all of our stories"), but I do want to tell you about something my now-husband told me then that helped me begin my healing process.

When I was deep in the Twilight Zone, I was absolutely spinning my wheels in a big pile of shame-sh*t. There really isn't another way to put that more politely and have you understand the depth of how I was judging myself. Scott looked at me one day and said, "Carleen, you need put your damn suitcases down." I looked at him quizzically, not knowing what in the world he was talking about.

He said, "It's like this. You have these suitcases. You wake up in the morning, and right away when you get out of bed, you pick them up and carry them with you to the bathroom. You set them down while you take a shower, and then you carry them over to the sink while you brush your teeth and do the rest of your morning routine. Then you carry them downstairs and set them in the kitchen while you get breakfast."

Okay . . .

"Then you lug them out to the car and drive to work. When you get to work, you carry them in with you. You set them by your desk. And then you carry them with you to your classroom and set them down there. And then you go to lunch. Guess what? You take your suitcases with you. You even take them with you when you go to the bathroom."

Christmas 2018. To get it, I had to make threats. There was only one photo where we were all looking at the camera. This was it! (#Lili)

I'm starting to see a pattern . . .

"Pretty soon, it's time to leave work, so you lug those bags out to the car. You go to the gym, and you carry those bags in with you. Then back out to the car. You stop at the grocery store and bring them with you—in and out. Then it's time for you to cook dinner. You set the bags on the counter. You move them over to the table when it's time to eat. Then to the kitchen again to do dishes. Then you move them to the couch when you sit down to watch TV or grade papers. Now it's time to go to bed—gotta brush your teeth and take off your makeup—and you take those bags with you. Now it's time to go to sleep, so you set those bags down at the foot of your bed. And guess what? They're still there the next morning. And then you start all over again."

Matthew's golden birthday trip to AT&T Park to watch his San Francisco Giants. #Buster! (#Lini)

Damn.

"Aren't you tired?"

Exhausted.

"Carleen . . . those bags belong to you. They will always belong to you. But you do not need to carry them with you all day, every day. It's okay for you to put them up in the closet and LEAVE THEM THERE. Yes, there will be times when you will open that closet and look at those bags and think about where they came from, but then you have to shut the door and leave them there. You are not doing any good for yourself or for anyone else if you are carrying those bags around with you 24/7. Put. Down. Your. Damn. Suitcases!"

That conversation was one of the most poignant moments of my life. Here was someone who was looking at all my faults—all the darkest darks of my life—and he still saw my light. And he wanted ME to see my own light. I'm not sure I would be where I am now if he had not said that to me at that exact moment. It—and he—are brilliant.

Sisters, if you are carrying something with you everywhere, stop. Just STOP. Stop carrying that experience with you. I know it's really, really hard to let go of it if you feel bad about it. I've been where you are. I've put my suitcases away successfully for a while, and then I've gone back and picked them up again to study them. But then I remember what Scott told me, and I do everything I can to shove them back in the closet. It doesn't mean I don't remember they're there (or that someone won't remind me they're there—sigh), but I am better able to focus on my life and the business of helping others if I'm not carrying them with me all the time.

We women have been conditioned to judge ourselves a million different ways already. Sisters, don't add to the Shame Sh*tshow. It's powerful enough already. Stop using it as ammunition against yourself. Own your story, yes. But stop weighing yourself down with an anvil. Forgive yourself. The quality of your life and the good that you will be able to do in the world depends on it.

> "Owning our story can be hard, but not nearly as difficult as spending our lives running from it. Embracing our vulnerabilities is risky but not nearly as dangerous as giving up on love and belonging and joy—the experiences that make us the most vulnerable. Only when we are brave enough to explore the darkness will we discover the infinite power of our light." (*The Gifts of Imperfection*)

Damn, Brené is good. And so are you. Believe it.

Idea #2: Looking at Where You've Been to See Where You're Headed

There is wisdom in knowing when to look behind you or in front of you.

Take driving, for example. You have a big windshield that shows you the expanse of land that lies before you, the road on which you are traveling, what's coming at you, and so forth. When you first start driving, it's easy to slip into looking at the road directly in front of you to make sure you are keeping the car between the lines and far enough away from the car in front of you. If you do that all the time, however, you might miss your turn or not see a deer that has decided to cross the highway in front of you. As time goes on, you get better and better at scanning back and forth, taking in your surroundings, and making informed decisions about what to do next.

Your windshield is nice and big for a reason: there's a lot to see and a lot to think about to be a successful, defensive driver. But of course, you also have mirrors to see where you've been and what might be coming up behind you. You certainly do NOT want to keep your eyes fixed on your rearview mirror, especially when you're going 70 mph down the freeway! That would be absolute madness (unless, for some reason, you decided to drive your car backwards, which is a whole other thing).

However, you DO want to occasionally peek at your mirrors because what you see can affect your trip. The same concept applies to life, especially when it comes to owning and telling our stories. Rockstar storyteller Kevin Kling echoes the sentiments of Brené Brown when he says, "The minute I tell a story, it doesn't control me anymore."

Now, the two of us are 100 percent guilty of repeating stories. Twenty-plus years of teaching gives a person lots of practice telling a story with JUST the right details (which is super helpful when working with teenagers). It also happens when we want to remember something beautiful or funny, when we want to help or entertain someone, and when we want to reveal something about ourselves to those who have earned the right to know our stories.

But what about the particularly difficult stories? Isn't it dangerous to get stuck in them and their destructive power? Shouldn't we leave them in the past and focus on the present moment or a promising future? As we said in the previous section, absolutely, yes—that is, if the storytelling is rooted in shame. We should not repeat difficult stories if doing so keeps us

trapped in that negative energy loop that turns storytelling into a mind-numbing, depressive drug that has the capability to hollow us out and rip us to shreds.

However, if we find we have given control back to a destructive story at some point (perhaps after looking at our suitcases for too long), we may find ourselves in need of a booster shot of storytelling, either to ourselves or to our trusted team members. One immunization doesn't always do the trick, so #GetYourBooster, people.

The key to making this work is reflection. Here are a few creative activities to figure out what your brain has to say about where you've been. There are many others, of course—these are just a few of our favorites.

1. **Timeline Activity.** Those of you who tend to order your thinking in a more linear or chronological way might find this activity helpful. Start by creating a list of the top ten BEST things that have happened to you and another list of the top ten WORST things that have happened to you. These do not need to be big events, by any means—just gather the examples you feel have affected you the most.

   Try to get a sense for when each of these things happened chronologically. Then, create an X/Y axis graph on a piece of paper. Your X axis should represent time in years, and your Y axis should represent intensity (+/- 10 in each direction). Plot out your twenty events on the graph and connect the dots until you have something that looks like a heartbeat. You can dress it up with doodles if you like.

   Then, put down your #SpecialPens and look at the picture you've created. What patterns do you see? What connections can you make? Are there any trends? Are there events you forgot about that you feel you need to add? What does this timeline tell you about yourself? What can you learn from it as you move forward?

   This activity is also powerful if you overlay other people's timelines on top of yours. Do you see any similarities? Are there places where your story diverged in one direction and the other person's went another way? How did that affect your relationship? Did something on someone else's timeline have an effect on yours? Have you had similar experiences to someone else's? What can you learn from one another? Did anything in another person's way-back history affect them later in life—and THEN affect you because you are in a relationship with them?

2. **Mindmapping.** Those of you who are visual but have more thematic minds might enjoy

this activity. Mindmapping is all about exploring not only the organization of a central idea but also the connections that might exist between ideas. Start by writing down the central idea you want to explore in the middle of a piece of paper. It could be an event, a person's name, or even just a feeling (like joy). Put a shape around the word.

Two of my Concordia College besties, Jessica and Wendi. We had lots of fun PG-13 adventures. (#Lini)

Next, think about whether you can break that idea down into another layer of ideas. If we use the joy example, you might think of people who bring you joy, experiences that bring you joy, food that brings you joy, and so forth. Write those secondary ideas around the central idea in a different color and draw a shape around them. Connect those shapes back to the central shape.

Amy and I rocking our color block outfits in college. We were bomb diggety! (#Lili)

Then, look at each of your secondary ideas and see if you can break them down even further into a third layer. For example, you could list the names of the people who bring you joy, draw a shape around them, and connect them back. Then you could add a layer of characteristics of each person that bring you joy, or experiences you've had together, and so on. This process can go as deep as you want it, and you can doodle and color-code to your heart's content.

The magic happens when you lay your #SpecialPens down and look for patterns. You might make visual connections from one side of the map to the other! Self-knowledge will pop off the page and might help you not only understand yourself, but also figure out what you need to do in similar situations in the future.

3. **Layered Collaging.** This activity may be most appealing to people who would rather be a little less organized with their idea-gathering process. Gather up some magazines, a big piece of paper, a pair of scissors, and some tape or glue. Spend some time kicking it Old School by flipping through magazines looking for images, colors, patterns, and words or phrases that speak to you. Don't think too hard about it; just rip a bunch of stuff out at the beginning without a lot of judgement or evaluation.

When you feel like you have a lot to work with, look at everything you've gathered. Trim,

arrange, layer, and stick it all down in a way that feels pleasing to you. Don't think too much about what you're doing—just let it flow. Then look for the patterns and connections and listen to what they might tell you.

Some people like to start this activity with an intention for its outcome—like, "What can I learn about the role my parents played in my life?" Other people like to do the activity without a specific intention to see what their subconscious wants to tell them. Whatever method you choose, let your creative mind say what it needs to say.

Idea #3: Feel the Feels in a Place Where You Belong

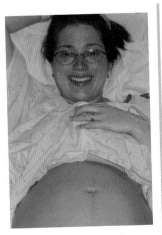

This was bed rest week one. Kiddo was raring to go at thirty-two weeks. That first night, I kept trying to tell the doctors that this was not possible because second semester was starting the next day....and I had a brand new group of kids to teach. The docs won—I stayed. She was born at four pounds, two ounces after bed rest week two. (#Lili)

We women have traditionally been made to feel like we shouldn't openly express what's bothering us. Suck it up! Stop crying! Deal with it! There are people who have it worse than you! Show no weakness! We don't have time for this! We don't want to hear you cry! Be strong! Be happy! Put a smile on your face!

We don't know about you, but our intense emotions tend to leak out of our eyes, no matter what we're feeling. Intense happiness? Tears. Intense frustration? Tears. Intense anger? Tears. Intense pride about our kiddos? Tears. Tears aren't helpful in all situations, especially when we are interacting with people who see them as a sign of weakness. (WE don't think they are, and YOU might not think they are, but there are, sadly, people out there who do.)

If you're like us, you probably end up stuffing your feelings in an emotional lockbox to get through whatever you have to get through. But just because you stuff them doesn't mean all that energy disappears, so you might need to give yourself a chance to let it out in a healthy way so it doesn't beat you up from the inside out.

Make sure your space and the company you keep feel safe to you. You might want to do this by yourself, but you can also do it with trusted people who won't freak out if you freak out.

What to do? You could . . .

- Crank up the music in your car or in your living room and SING ALONG AT THE TOP OF

YOUR LUNGS.
- Do something super physical, like run, kickbox, lift weights, or do power yoga (that's no joke!)—and MAKE SOME NOISE, even if it's just heavy exhalation.
- Have a healthy cry—and vocalize what you are feeling. If it helps, SCREAM THOSE FEELS.
- Do something exhilarating, like riding a rollercoaster— and TELL THE WORLD HOW YOU FEEL ABOUT IT!

Then, after you feel the feels, sit with them for a while. Let peace, quiet, and love seep into the space you just created with movement and sound. Let them fill you up and soothe you, and then rise up and get back to your life, stronger and more whole than you were before.

House-big with The Boy (™). I loved being preggers! My dad kills me in this one. Also, those were my Indestructo Pants. (#Lini)

Carleen: I experienced this during the Twilight Zone Era. I was about ready to BURST from the stress of my situation, and I could hardly keep it together around people. It was absolutely maddening because I didn't want to lose it and make people think I was crazy, but I also got to the point where I couldn't hold it in anymore.

One night, after Matthew's dad picked him up, I sat alone in my living room in front of the fireplace and started to cry. I knew there was no one around to hear me (well, let's just say I hope the neighbors were out of earshot), so I just let loose. I ended up working myself up to the point where I started screaming at the top of my lungs—I turned the anger/frustration dial up to eleven. As I sat there and listened (I was literally ecstatic), I heard myself become positively primal. I had NO IDEA I had that much in me to release, and I had to just get out of my own way. And when I was done, I was done. No one had to know about it, I didn't hurt anyone or myself, and I felt so much better afterward.

Lisa: When I went through the decline of my second marriage, I kept it on the down-low. For a while, I was not even confiding in my mom . . . which is not a thing. I figured I should be able to handle my sh*t. I sat with the stress and sat with it and sat with it until one morning when I walked into the world language office. One of my colleagues said good morning and asked me how I was. How was I? I was at my tipping point, and I burst into a fountain of tears. Steady, even-tempered, and solid Lisa had a complete and total meltdown. Right there in the office. I am not sure how I pulled myself together to teach that day, but I did it. Perhaps it was the release in that place where I belonged that I needed to move forward.

We're not saying this strategy is going to cure what ails you, necessarily, but it is a way to release an emotional pressure valve, after which you might be able to #GetUpAndTryAgain much faster.

Idea #4: Goodbye Ceremonies

Grief and loss are an undeniable part of life. Every one of us will experience them, whether we want to or not, and we have to find our way through the stages of grieving. This takes time, which can be disruptive to our lives. While we as humans could do a better job of normalizing loss, societal rules do exist that govern this experience for most people—as long as the loss is seen as "normal," like a death of a loved one or the loss of a job.

But what happens when we experience a loss that doesn't fit into a neat package and doesn't follow the rules?

Psychology has a term for it: disenfranchised grief. To be disenfranchised means to be denied a right or privilege (like disenfranchised voters), so if you are experiencing disenfranchised grief, you might experience a loss that may be unrecognized or even deemed unacceptable by society, even if it completely blows up your life.

Kenneth Doka came up with this term back in the mid-1980s and wrote about it in his book, *Disenfranchised Grief: New Directions, Challenges, and Strategies for Practice.* According to Doka, disenfranchised grief fits this description if:

1. Society deems the relationship unimportant, so therefore the grief is not acknowledged (such as miscarriages, the death of a pet, or the death of an ex-spouse).
2. The death is stigmatized by society (such as suicide, accidental drug overdose, or

My last goodbye to the sauna ("sow-na") my dad designed and built in my childhood home. Lake Vermilion rocks give off the best steam (no, the stove isn't on). I miss it so much! (#Lini)

Just So You Know . . .

#EXTRA Life Lessons:
If Carleen gets quiet, look for her in the sauna. Actually, don't. Don't look for her in the sauna. If Lisa gets quiet, expect a llama kick.
#ThoseEyebrowsTho

abortion).

3. The relationship is stigmatized by society (such as the death of a partner from an extra-marital affair or a drinking buddy).

4. The loss is not a death, so it is not recognized as a grief-worthy (such as dementia, a relationship with a friend or family member that has ended, or religious conversion).

Grief and loss are complicated enough—but if your grief is disenfranchised, you might feel more isolated and disconnected, and less supported. You might feel like you have to keep your grief hidden, or at the very least, you can't talk about it much for fear of judgement from the outside. There may be people who tell you your experience "isn't really a thing," that you should just get over it already, or that you are in the wrong for having these feelings.

But grief and loss, disenfranchised or not, are still grief and loss. They affect us. They change us. And you as a human being deserve the space and love to get through it, find closure, and move on.

This is one of those things that might be good to work through with a therapist (as we established earlier, we are not professionals!). But we can speak from experience that engaging in goodbye ceremonies either within a trusted, supported group or by yourself can really help, especially if you are not able to take part in closure rituals like a funeral. It can also be helpful if you experience something that feels like a death, such as the end of a meaningful relationship.

Let's say your relationship with someone has gone completely south, and nothing you've tried has brought it back. That person hasn't died, per se, but the person who had a positive impact on your life has, in a way, and you need to mourn the loss of that person. You could write a goodbye letter to the version of that person and thank them for everything they did to make your life wonderful. You don't have to send this letter; the act of just writing it can be the closure ritual your psyche needs to move forward.

Another example might be choosing a plant to put in a meaningful place to honor your grief and symbolize the new life that invariably comes after letting go. The type of plant might be symbolic in some way. You could even go one step further and bury something at the base of that plant, performing something akin to a mini funeral. Whatever you do might feel like forgiveness of some sort, if that's what you need.

Whatever you choose, we recommend it be important to you, appropriate for the situation, and positive in nature, if at all possible. (But if you need to do something a titch destructive

to, let's say, acknowledge the release of something harmful/toxic/traumatic, we won't judge. Just don't hurt anyone or yourself in the process. Or do anything illegal.)

Idea #5: Oils We Like for This

Jasmine
Neroli
Palo Santo
Roman Chamomile

Rule #4

GET UP AND TRY AGAIN.

Chapter Sixteen

WHEN YOU'RE READY, YELL "GO!"

Dear Lovelies,

So, there you are, sitting in the water.

The wipeout is over, your swimsuit has gone as far up your butt as it's going to go (this time), your lifejacket is all up in your armpits, and your skis may or may not be within reach. You wiggle your feet (good, you still have both of them), you move your head side to side (good, you didn't crush your spine), and you let out something like "OPE" (good, you still have teeth and a tongue and no obvious sign of brain damage). The boat is circling around, and pretty soon the tow rope is going to go right by you. What are you going to do?

You have a few options:

1. Lie there and be grateful. You know . . . raise your face to the sky, let the sun's warmth hit you, and thank your guardian angel or whoever just saved you from DYING for looking out for you one more time. Hey . . . look at that. Blue sky. There are those puffy clouds you love so much. And there's a dragonfly. Hi, little buddy.

2. Cry/weep/wail. Flail your arms. Yell to the boat to hurry up and get the hell over here so your spotters can get you out of the water, wrapped up in a towel, and back to shore. Swear at your stupid skis that never fit right in the first place. Curse yourself for ever thinking you could walk on water like Jesus. (Who do you think you are, anyway?) Rue the day your swimsuit even THINKS about hurting you like that again. Complain as you get in the boat. Sulk and pout all the way back to the shore. Wipe away the snot that's running down your nose. Stomp past everyone on your way up to the cabin to change into pants.

3. Laugh—loudly. Wonder if anyone caught that one on camera. Think, now THAT was a Wipeout for the Ages . . .

4. Think back over what you were doing right before you wiped out. Are you still getting the hang of it? Were you trying a new trick? Is there an adjustment you need to make next time? Was there a rogue wave that tripped you up? Is something wrong with the boat? Are you too tired to be skiing right now—do you need a break? Did you stiffen up or lean too far one way or the other? Were you distracted by something? Is the weather a little iffy right now? Should you wait for the waves to die down a little bit? Did the wipeout just . . . happen?

This was a first day of ninth grade selfie! Kiddo was starting a new school, and Mama Llama was nervous. (#Lili)

5. Get your feet in the skis again. Get the hair out of your face. Grab the rope. Give it a tug to gather some slack. Grab the handle before the boat gets into position. Let your skis rise up and get the rope centered between them. Take a deep breath and relax. Find your balance point. Make sure your knees are bent slightly. Bend your arms just so. Tell yourself, "All right. I can do this. Give me just one more minute—then I'll try again."

Scott, Matthew, and Dean on Father's Day at the baseball field. We've actually got this coparenting thing down. #Grateful (#Lini)

6. Grab your skis if you can; if you can't, just let them float. Tell the driver you're done for now so he or she can switch into recovery mode instead of gearing up for the next attempt. Let your spotter scoop your skis and the rope out of the water. Climb the ladder. Wrap yourself in a towel and settle into the seat—put your feet up. Marvel at the power of the motor as it growls to life and steadfastly grinds through the water to bring you home. Feel the wind in your hair.

Lots of self-help books might tell you there are right choices and wrong choices on that list. Some self-help books might make you guess which one is the right answer (and when you guess wrong, they'll make you feel a little sheepish or . . . dumb). Some self-help books might try to trick you into THINKING that one answer is best and then pull the rug out from under you (which really makes you feel stupid).

By now, you know that this is not your typical self-help book.

There really isn't a right answer to the question, "What are you going to do next?" because there are a lot of variables at play, like how you're feeling, what the weather's like, how high the sun is in the sky, whether you're hurt or not, and so on. And there are times when each of these reactions would be appropriate (even #2, because those emotions have got to play themselves out, right?). (Just know if you do #2, you might annoy others a little, but whatever, they can deal—they aren't the ones with the recent memory of a swimsuit migrating too far north.)

Now, we highly recommend the options that end with you getting up to try again . . . we're optimists, after all (and that's what Cedric's final Rule for Life as Illustrated by Waterskiing is all about).

But hey . . . if you don't wanna, then don't! Or if you want to take some time to recover before you give it another go, do that! Or maybe getting up and trying again means next time, you're going to try wakeboarding, kayaking, floating on a floaty, or just putting your toes in the water from the shore . . . whatever! You are honestly golden in our eyes, whichever way you go.

It's really not about which decision you make, anyway—it's about you taking the time to MAKE the decision instead of leaving it up to someone else. You call the shots, Sister. Not the boat, not the spotter, and certainly not anyone else.

Just remember that if you do decide to give it another go, yell "GO!" when you're ready (and not a second before).

BFF,
Lisa and Carleen

P.S. I (Carleen) seriously used to imagine the boat motor was alive when I was a kid. It was a friendly monster that I shouldn't try to hug. I mean, yes, it was the key to my ultimate happiness, but it could also kill me (which goes to show you, love the boat, but respect its power).

Chapter Seventeen

LISA STORIES

The Warrior Princess of Edgewood Vista

Don't let that sweet face fool you! Little girlfriend did not fall far from the tree! (#Lili)

It is only fitting that Kiddo learned to walk using her Great-Grandma Bert's walker. Grandma Bert was the strong-as-hell matriarch of our branch of the family until she passed in 2009, at the age of ninety-six. My Uncle Vern used to refer to Grandma Bert and her sister, my Great Aunt Erna, as tough old girls! And they were! When Kiddo was young, she got ahold of Grandma Bert's walker, and was quickly cruising around visiting anyone in the vicinity. After that, it wasn't a huge leap for her to walk on her own! Grandma Bert is the start of my family's long line of strong independent women. I could write a whole chapter on resiliency with Grandma Bert and Aunt Erna stories. Their stories are very humbling and would likely make you cry. So, when I think I just can't even, it would behoove me to think of them. Big girl panties: put 'em ON!

So, Kiddo was born seven weeks early at four pounds two ounces. She was so tiny, but so strong! She was out of NICU in one week and out of the hospital in two. I was supposed to be having two baby showers instead of giving birth that weekend, but hey, we just rolled with it because whatcha gonna do? We baby showered! We had one of the showers in the hospital community rooms. You know, because it was the day after I had given birth. The joke has always been that Kiddo didn't want to miss the party!

By the time Kiddo was born, Grandma Bert was already living at Edgewood Vista, an assisted

living facility in Minot. When you think Superhero, your first thought is probably not Disney Princess, but don't let her Snow White dress fool you. This kid was a warrior princess! She never needed to be saved, because she always did the saving.

Kiddo was always comfortable at Edgewood Vista. I had never seen a toddler work a crowd like she did. She was so warm, open, and not scared of the elderly as some children are. She had a light and joy about her, and even the crabbiest person was powerless to her great big, sweet smile!

Every time we visited Edgewood Vista, we'd race to find Grandma. Most of the time we'd find her in her room, and then we'd move to the great room where we could sit at a table or find a comfortable sofa. Kiddo loved spending time with Grandma. She'd also go up to anyone and everyone with a huge grin and open arms.

Because of Kiddo's warmth, she ended up adopting an elderly man named Bill. He was so kind, and he adored her! As soon as Kiddo found Grandma, she would then go find Bill. It was beautiful. Because his kids and grandkids all lived in different states, he seemed quite lonely. Whether or not Kiddo sensed this loneliness, she indeed picked him, and our visits always brightened his day! He always asked her questions, always had a piece of candy in his pocket for her, and always had a hug waiting.

My first and only has reached out and affected people in a profound way for such a little human. Being able to break down barriers and communicate is one of her superpowers. It's not always easy to do, and I am so proud I get to be her mama!

Lisa vs Missouri Synod

It was 1992 and Paul and I were reviewing our vows for our upcoming wedding. I noticed my vows included the verbiage that I would obey my husband. I did not notice any similar verbiage for him. So, I said either we both said it or neither of us was going to say it. After a couple of rounds with our pastor, he gave in and let me remove them from my vows. I was ready to walk straight to another church. Under no circumstance were those words going to come out of my mouth. Missouri Synod was strict, but I was ornery!

As an adult, I changed churches a few times. Eventually I stopped going. Part of it was because I was REALLY mad at God for my messed-up adulthood and the losses I suffered. And part of it was that I was so tired and the idea of getting up and going somewhere on a Sunday

morning was truly repulsive (it still is).

I am still spiritual and have a personal relationship with God. But I need to do it my way now (or maybe forever). My "Religion" has morphed into me being a mix of Buddhist and Christian who loves healing crystals and Pixie Dust. No matter how anyone feels about my religious life and my choices (because truly, isn't it between me and God?), I would tell them this is self-care and it's important. Because what good are you to yourself or anyone else if you are falling apart?

So, in case you are wondering, this is how it is with me and my God.

My religion is a hug from my kid.
My religion is falling asleep holding my husband's hand.
My religion is a snuggle with my pets.
My religion is a sunset over the water.
My religion is watching birds on our bird feeder.
My religion is the sound of mourning doves.
My religion is my favorite music.
My religion is running around the lake first thing in the morning and being in peaceful commune with my God.
My religion is yoga.
My religion is giving people the benefit of the doubt.
My religion is being kind.
My religion is teaching.
My religion is listening to my guides.
My religion is my Forever Friends.
My religion is my family.
My religion is helping others.
My do unto others? Don't be a dick.
I bet Jesus felt the same way.
I understand the Bible . . . well, as much as anyone
can . . . I get the central meaning.
I know what it means to be a good person.
I live by His word.
I just don't worship in a church with other people.
Because churches are too peopley.

#SweetBubbaKisses (#Lili)

Don't judge. You might need to do a religious reset one day. Instead, listen to the tape that plays in your head. Whose voice is it? Is it even yours? Who are you living for? Which things in your life are serving you and which aren't? Look at what's detrimental to your story and get rid of it. You get a do-over every single day when you get out of bed. Be intentional! Make it count!

My Spirit Guides

I didn't know what spirit guides were until I accidentally found one in Elizabeth Gilbert. (For those of you who don't know, she's an amazing writer.) She was revolutionary to me. I felt like a miserable, stuck failure during the end of my second marriage. She helped me realize I was neither and that I had choices. That I needed to act. But I wanted to keep my family together. I did not want my child to be from a broken home. I wanted to give her better than that. So I kept things hidden from friends and family because if I talked about it, it was real. And I didn't want it to be real.

The ironic thing is that Kiddo's dad discovered Elizabeth first. He saw her on *Oprah,* thought that I would like her story, and introduced me to her writing. But we were each journeying on our own path, and we couldn't walk together any longer. I was tired. I was broken. And I needed to take myself back. It was a hard fall, but I'm like a Weeble. I don't knock down easily. And my four-year-old daughter was watching me. So, falling apart in front of her? Not an option. Between my mother, his mother, and Elizabeth Gilbert, they were all indispensable at keeping me together.

Glennon Doyle is my second spirit guide, speaking to me on the same level as Liz. I knew she was a Soul Sister after reading the first paragraph of her first book. I don't voraciously read books, but I devoured Liz and Glennon. And the *Outlander* series, obviously, because Jamie. Duh.

Because the past two years of my little family's life had been an unmitigated hell (things happened to each of the three of us in that time period that would bring anyone to their damn knees), I hadn't been keeping up with my guides. In April 2018 I learned that Glennon had divorced her husband and married Abby Wambach, which blew my freaking mind (we are a soccer family). And Elizabeth had divorced and was in a relationship with her best friend Rayya, who was suffering from cancer. Elizabeth says this about her divorce and subsequent relationship: "For those of you who are doing the math here, and who are wondering if this situation is why my marriage came to an end this spring, the simple answer is yes. (Please

understand that I cannot say anything more about it than that. I trust you are all sensitive enough to understand how difficult this has been. As David Foster Wallace once wrote: 'The truth will set you free—but not until it's had its way with you.' Yes, it has been hard. Yes, the truth has had its way with us. And yes, the truth still stands.)"

This is a woman who I admire. And she's not apologizing for her life. I look at her life and her loves. This woman I adore. And I no longer feel sheepish about my failed marriages. Deep down, I have never really felt sheepish. I had zero options. But comments that have been made and the way society looks at someone with my track record . . . well, it's just hurtful. (And why the hell is my life reduced to the phrase "track record"? I call bullsh*t!) For those who judge me? Do what you need to do. I pay you no mind. And when things happen to you that are out of your control, I will not judge you. I'll never judge you. And if you need me, I will be here for you.

Elizabeth's news affected me about as profoundly as Doug's quote did. After Rayya passed, Liz wrote, "There is no love that can ever replace Rayya's love, of course . . . but that doesn't mean the Universe won't keep trying its hardest to fill that hole in my heart with grace and friendship and kindness and goodness." She also said, "To be a human, it seems to me, is the greatest and most ridiculous and most painful and most beautiful incarnation in town. You never know what's coming. It's terrifying at times, but I'll take it. I'll take the whole ride."

Know what? I would do it all again—all the pain, all the suffering, all the things. I have no regrets about anyone I've loved and with whom I have spent time. I'd like to negotiate tweaking a few things here and there, but I would experience the atomic bombs going off again because something beautiful was created in each experience. I learned something valuable each time. I had a deep, loving connection with another human each time, and it's a great fortune to fall in love and be loved back.

Thank you, Liz, for the validation and the reminder that healing always returns to fill the empty space.

Recurring Problem: No Cure

I have been mostly stubbornly happy since my late twenties. I have frustrated and perplexed people with my steadfast loyalty to the idea that you can be happy most of the time. My idea of happiness is not jumping up and down with joy every minute of every day; rather, it's an oasis of peace, calm, and tranquility you can create in either a physical or spiritual sense inside your head or in your home.

I have never understood people who don't think this is possible. Who wants to perpetuate a sh*tshow inside your own home? Now, children and teenagers are a different story. We need to help them through their hard times. But adults? Come on, man! I try to pull it together, try to stay positive, and try to look for the lessons. If I don't, I would be a full sh*tshow participant. I have the depression and anxiety thing legit and diagnosed, but I try to be the role model and set the stage for myself and my family. Emphasis on try. Have I failed at this? Yes, all. The. Damn. Time. But I try to give my loved ones the benefit of the doubt and I try to take care of myself.

If I were my own best friend, I would say, "Hey, you have to do this, because if you go down, you are useless to yourself and others." You know the saying: If Mama ain't happy, ain't nobody happy. I am still not good at pitfalls and avoiding going from 0 to 60 when my buttons get pushed. But the way I have survived life's curveballs, and how I'm still surviving my adult life, is focusing on happiness. I can only control myself. My thoughts. My actions. This is my life and my mindset. I am totally imperfect, I screw up all the time, but the happiness mindset is what I strive for. It's what helps me get up after I fall. Also, my parents. Always my parents.

Netflix and . . . Netflix

During the summer of 2014, I was not fine, mental health wise. It had been a great year at school. Kiddo didn't have any significant issues that summer. Kris was working during the day. And I had all kinds of time to do all kinds of things. Know what I did? After dropping Kiddo off at day camp, I binged-watched Netflix until it was time to pick her up. I did this for several weeks. No one knew what I was doing because I was the only one home. Now, granted, *Big Love* is awfully addicting, but I started to feel a little funky about myself. My binge-watching wasn't anything I was willing to share with my spouse, so that indicated it was likely a problem. I was using it as an escape . . . but there was nothing tangible I was escaping from. I knew I did not want to go back on meds. I know Western medicine is necessary at times. After all, I have to take meds for high blood pressure so my kidneys don't fail. But I did NOT want to add more pharmaceuticals to the mix.

Two things happened that summer. The first was realizing that if I didn't want to go back on meds for anxiety and depression, I would need to get off my ass and do something radical. The second was that my friend, Lora, came into town from Minot to be with her dad in the hospital. Lora is one of my oldest and dearest friends. She wanted to get together, but the prospect of leaving my five-mile radius was horrifying. I was emotionally paralyzed. I couldn't do it. But I had to because Lora is my good friend and I needed to BE a good friend.

Lora and me circa 1984. DIY Halloween costumes! SO '80s! (#Lili)

So I thought about this for four days. Three days. Two days. She's gonna be here tomorrow. Day. Of. It was a Friday. I was a deer in headlights, but didn't want to be a total derp. There was a box of essential oils sitting by the door. They had been sitting there for four months. I saw people post about oils that might be able to help in my private oily Facebook group. I thought, "Well, I've got nothing to lose. It's this or meds." So, I dug in the box and picked out four oils that people had recommended. I put them all on at the same time on different areas of my body. Within 20 minutes I felt like a different PERSON. Like me, but different! Familiar. The me I used to be. The me I was accustomed to being. The me everyone knew me to be. The me that I was supposed to be!

I texted Lora and told her I could pick her up for lunch (leave the house?) at the hospital (drive INTO the city?). We would eat lunch at one of my favorite places and then I'd drop her back off (WTH is happening?). But before any of this happened, I grabbed Kiddo and suggested heading over to Toys "R" Us to use my Groupon before it expired (who the hell AM I?). All of this normally would have been fine, but because of my "bad season" for the previous several weeks, it seemed monumental. So, we did all that and . . . it was fine! I felt great, and I didn't let my friend down! I wasn't tired, I wasn't crabby, and I wasn't emotionally paralyzed!

As soon as I got home, I called Kris and told him what happened! Of course, then I had to tell him about the binge-watching, but whatever. Being a skeptic and a realist, he suggested it could be the placebo effect. Yes, it totally could have been a placebo effect. But whatever it was that happened was still working one week, two weeks, two months, and almost five years later.

I've gotta tell you, the idea of using an oil for something other than cooking or in my car seemed weird. I was resistant at first because it didn't make sense to me. But what I knew for sure was that I needed to make a change. For me, on that day, that meant trying essential oils. Shout-out to my sister, Michelle, for introducing them to me! It has been a game changer for me and my family and I've never looked back. That summer, I needed a growth mindset. I needed to step outside my box, get outside my comfort zone. I had to do something, because doing nothing was NOT an option. I put on my oils (not baby oil, '80s girls—how did we EVER think THAT was a good idea) and GOT back on my SKIS!

Chapter Eighteen

CARLEEN STORIES

The Scratch and Dent Blues

2018 was the year I got old.

I say this with my tongue firmly planted in my cheek because I know that, based on the relative longevity in my family and the fact that I have not developed any super-significant health problems by the age of forty-seven, I am right smack in the middle of this crazy life.

However, my body has developed a whole bunch of *issues* that remind me I am no longer *young.* To say that my body is different after hysterectomy and menopause (I shall now say, "H&M," #BecauseShopping) is about the biggest understatement of the year . . . perhaps of the decade. I vaguely knew my body would change with age, but I didn't really KNOW HOW my body would change or TO WHAT EXTENT. No one told me. It was an abstract, far-away-in-the-future-so-why-worry-about-it-now concept. The future is now, people. The future is now. And it feels like a big, ol' hit-and-run sideswipe.

I've started to get used to the fact I'm not twenty anymore. Um, I'm not even THIRTY anymore. I'm getting darn close to not being FORTY anymore. And while I'm thankfully edging closer to accepting myself for me and saying to hell with societal beauty standards, there are still moments when the old, panicky feelings come back. They're now just more tired. :)

I should be over all of this, but I'm not. While it's true I don't freak out about it to the extent I used to, I will admit I still think about how I look now and then. Okay fine, I think about it every day. (But damn, it's hard to admit that while trying to come across as a strong woman who rises above.) I don't severely berate myself like I used to, but I still entertain the thought.

Aging usually comes as a reminder that everything is just a little bit . . . lower . . . and wider . . . than it used to be. It's in a colleague's voice in my head that after a certain age, it's more about how we cover things up than what we show off. It's in the comparison I make between my Current Self and my Self from a Few Years Ago, whom I liked better because she exercised and ate healthy and drank more water and . . . looked better.

I hate that I still critique myself because I know better—but you know what? It just happens. And then I have to run myself through the Intervention—you know, where you try to embrace every a-ha moment of every movie and documentary about appreciating what's on the inside of a person more than what's on the outside. I've been through that routine too many times to count. (Remember how we said sometimes life is circular? This is it, baby. This is it.)

For most of us, this issue goes waaaaay back, and it's not something that gets instantly fixed because you listen to a podcast or watch a video on YouTube. Nope—it still shows up, despite our best intentions to be liberated, strong, kick-ass women. What are we to do, then, when our insecurities decide to pull up a chair and stay a while instead of going out the window with your memory of where you left your keys?

At moments like these, it has helped me to face it HEAD ON and think/talk/write my way through it. If I don't do this, it's easy for me to get stuck in the panic cycle, and I end up A) wasting time, B) making myself and others miserable, C) missing out on something awesome, and D) getting a headache from crying, all of which I prefer to avoid.

I won't pretend thinking/talking/writing fixes everything, of course, but those activities get me to a place where I can consider what comes next . . . and there is always something better that comes after the storm passes.

The wisdom of aging has taught me that.

Here's an example.

My high school girlfriend and I used to sing the Body Blues when we were young and actually thought we were fat. (I see you nodding your head. Yup.) What follows is the Middle-Aged Version of that song entitled "The Scratch and Dent Blues." Read it, sing along, and add your own improvisation riff if you feel moved by the spirit. Weep with me, baby.

(Now, I have to do this with some humor—otherwise, I might ugly cry. I HATE to ugly cry be-

cause of my Stoopid Nose that runs like a stuck spigot because I broke it when I was twelve. No amount of sniffing works during Ugly Crying, so unless I have a tissue or ten around, I have to wipe the damn thing with my sleeve. Yeah, I'm that person. I know. Gross.)

The Scratch and Dent Blues

Words and Imaginary Music
by Carleen Matts-Behrends

1. When I sit cross-legged or on my knees for too long, I hobble like a troll for the first ten steps until my legs remember what the hell they're supposed to do. Every time, my darling husband asks me if I am okay. Yep. Just give me a minute . . .

2. Carrying a moderately heavy backpack or my crossbody purse for any significant length of time results in my left trapezius muscle tightening up like a boa constrictor that has been on a vegan diet for a year and a half.

3. Other things that bring on said trap pain: pushups. Planks. Five-pound weights (I used to do twenty). Sleeping funny. Grading papers. Breathing wrong. A gentle wind.

4. My legs look like a roadmap. Specifically, the entire East Coast. That is all.

Remember how we used to crinkle up tissue paper around the end of a pencil, dip it in Elmer's paste, and stick it on a cardstock cut-out of a butterfly in elementary school? Yeah, me too—I see something akin to that tissue paper every time I shrug my shoulders, bend my forearm just so, or forget to slather lotion on my hands. (Do they seriously call it crepe skin? Sigh . . .)

Lisa's Tow Rope . . . #NOPE

Lisa: So two days ago I pulled a wire—a pure white hair out of my throat. It was right in the middle, sticking straight OUT. And I can't express to you how hardcore it was. I'm pretty sure I could have used it to tow skiers behind the boat. Also, refusing to wash my hair for four to five days in a row is literally one of the most liberating things that I've ever done. LOVE YOU, DRY SHAMPOO!

Carleen: #DYING

*When things got you like . . .
NOPE! (#Lili)*

5. If I lie on my back in the grass too long, enjoying the swaying branches and the puffy-cloud-dotted blue sky above me, I must roll over on my side first before slowly pushing myself upright. (I learned that trick after my hysterectomy four years ago.)

6. My "cute" freckles have discovered one another and believe in the philosophy of strength in numbers. On my cheek. On my other cheek. Above my left eye. And on my upper lip. (No, honey, that's NOT dirt on my upper lip. No, it won't rub off. No, seriously . . . wait, you are actually going to wipe it? For real? See . . . no dirt. Nada.)

7. I have no uterus because it prolapsed and tried to follow Elvis out the building before my surgeon cut it off at the pass. (See what I did there?) As a result, I'm subconsciously terrified that something else in there is gonna fall down and won't be able to get up.

8. Sacral Colpopexy: look it up. While it assists in avoiding the aforementioned problem, it changes the WHOLE inner landscape. NOT ONE PERSON TOLD ME THIS WOULD HAPPEN. Poor husband must feel like a stranger in a strange land. At least he looks hot in camo.

9. It's sad but true . . . I have saggy butt cheeks. Yup. So much so, I think I've grown an extra half of one on each side. I do squats while I brush my teeth, but they just keep-a-sliding south. (Okay, I know I stole that joke from Lisa, but I think I should get to share it #BecauseCellulite.)

10. Cellulite. RATZER-FRATZER! Do you remember when yours came in? I do: summer 1994. That bastard is nothing if not loyal, not even taking a coffee break when I weighed 111 pounds on the Stress Diet. In fact, the two of us have almost made it to our silver anniversary. TBH? I wish it would leave me for a younger girl. On second thought, no. I love my younger Soul Sisters too much to stick them with him, but . . . geez. Enough now. Go away.

11. I have dry skin. I'm talking DRY SKIN, and it's literally EVERYWHERE. Some of you are totally saying, "Yep, I got you. I SO. GOT. YOU. It's a b*tch, ain't it?" Amen, sister. Amen.

12. Growing up, my mother fell asleep on the couch almost instantly when she finally sat down in the evening. We'd point our fingers and laugh and even take her picture (which was a commitment in the 1980s when we used film cameras). Guess who is following in her footsteps? Yep. Me. Out cold on the couch. Head bobbing. Mouth open and drooling at 9:00 p.m. At least I can instantly DELETE the digital pictures being taken of me instead of being surprised by them at the drug store photo counter. Sorry, Mom.

13. Three words: "poochy muffin top" (unless I lie on my back, in which case it converts to "pooling lava flow"). Where the HELL did that come from? Oh—that's right. My Stretchy-Stretchy, Pregnant Belly became My Loosey-Goosey, Tiger-Striped Belly. Then cupcakes. I love me some cupcakes. And if things don't "move" every day . . . well, sh*t.

14. There's a patch of skin right above my Baseball Mom sunglasses that apparently got too cozy with the sun and wrinkles up funny when I raise my eyebrows. I've also got UV damage that makes the skin around my mouth wrinkle up like cooked lasagna noodles if I try to look pouty in a picture. I'm not a smoker, so where did that come from? Does slurping coffee make wrinkles like that? Oh, it's the straws? Okay, well . . . pouting makes me look SO 2011 Instagram, so I'll just make another crazy face and call it good.

15. There's a crop of little hairs that stick straight up from my head, and they love to congregate in my part. Seeing them causes me to worry whether it's only a matter of time before I look like my DAD. I mean, welcome back, Little Ones—so glad you aren't gone for good . . . but did you really need to come back in GREY and ORNERY? Is this part of the reason why so many ladies cut their hair off when they reach a certain age? I think I might be onto something here . . . it has nothing to do with long hair being reserved for the younger ladies. Nope—I think it has EVERYTHING to do with being tired as HELL of dealing with those sh*tty little hairs.

16. I eat pretty well. I really do (besides the occasional cupcake #BecauseCupcakes). I eat fruits, veggies, healthy fats, protein . . . all in appropriate portion sizes. But if I even look SIDEWAYS at anything with too much sugar (#Cupcakes), I swear it jumps straight from my grubby little hands right onto my thighs like a giant chigger.

Oh, I could go on . . . and on . . . and on. I know this list is going to grow with time, and it freaks me out. Then there's the horror of comprehending the ramifications of gaining five pounds a year (which doesn't seem that bad until you do the math of what a decade could do).

It feels too soon for all this to be happening because my SPIRIT doesn't feel that old. My spirit wants to jump up and plant a smooch on everyone's cheek (but I won't do that because not everyone welcomes an attack from the #AwkwardFlamingo). My spirit wants to march right back into kickboxing class (even though I haven't seriously done it post H&M #BecauseBellyBloat) and work out my emotions on an imaginary target. My spirit wants to get up on the table and DAAAAANCE!

Yet, I struggle to put on freshly washed jeans after a shower and subsequent lotion.

One night in June 2018, I saw a performance by Cirque Montage, which is made up of jugglers, aerialists, gymnasts, and other amazing people who do crazy things with their bodies. The craziest was a contortionist who moved her body in ways we thought weren't humanly possible. She bent herself in half the opposite way.

There are times when I can't bend forward far enough to reach my toes without relocating an organ or two! She balanced her entire body weight on ONE HAND—and spun around!

I trip on a shiny, tiled floor and then look around to see if there's anything I can blame! (Okay, I'm looking to see if anyone saw.)

She shot an arrow at a target with her FEET— and hit it! And—she was bent in half BACK-WARDS!

I can barely throw a paper towel into the garbage can at close range without pulling a muscle!

Holy sh*t!

But none of that made me feel bad about myself. You know why? It was the look on her face. It was because she owned her body. It was because she was strong. It was because she looked BADASS . . . and she sent out a vibe that the rest of us could have our own version of #BADASSERY, even if we have cellulite!

The first time I set foot in Spain in 1996, I felt like I had lived there before. Like somehow a puzzle piece to my heart had just slid into place. Being able to go there again with Kris and Lauren (who was at camp in the Pyrenees) was priceless to me. (#Lili)

CPAP Love

Carleen: Optimism is using the wind from your husband's CPAP machine to cool down your night sweats.

Scott and me at niece/little sister Amy's wedding. Our family friend Lorraine teased him but good (and he teased her right back!). (#Lini)

Watching her, it dawned on me—I really don't know what my body can do post H&M. I haven't really taken the time to get to know her and her capabilities.

Sure, Current Post-H&M Self is not the same as Stress Diet Self, who went to the gym practically every day and wasn't carrying an extra 26.8 pounds (which is like 53.6 pounds on a short person) and drank her body weight in water instead of coffee. She's not the same woman who had all her hormones in a row, once upon a time—the one who didn't have to dress in layers because of the HOT FLASHES THAT POP UP OUT OF NOWHERE AT THE MOST INCONVENIENT TIMES, ESPECIALLY WHEN I'D RATHER SLEEP SOUNDLY THAN WAKE UP IN A POOL OF BACK SWEAT.

Current Self is NOT the same . . . but how do I know she's not better? I don't know. I haven't bothered to find out.

Yep, I could spend more of my time singing "The Scratch and Dent Blues." I'm female and a human, so I know I will do precisely that, again and again. Also, "The Scratch and Dent Blues" can be quite beautiful because when you start hearing the "Amens" in the audience, you know you aren't the only one struggling. But the blues is not the only kind of music out there, and I have to remind myself that it's okay to change the chord and the channel.

If I change the channel and really LISTEN, it could be the perfect soundtrack for a long walk, for an Oula dance class, for yoga, for kayaking, and for a number of new experiences I haven't taken the time to explore.

You just have to approach it like putting on those freshly washed jeans after a shower and a slathering of lotion.

Prepare yourself. Take a deep breath. Shake that extra half booty into place. Jump up and down. Wiggle around as much as you must. Just get up and try again.

And now . . . a poem. Because poems are a nice way to wrap up Big Ideas.

Enough

Enough already.

ENOUGH!

WHEN will I relax and forgive myself for having flaws?

When will I dare to believe I'm holding up pretty well for a woman who is knocking on the door of fifty?

When will I stop thinking that in order to be a good catch, I have to be a composite of the best qualities of every hot woman I see in the media and at the gym—in other words, impossibly perfect?

How do we shrug off the toxic thoughts and allow ourselves to be happy?

Why do we allow our value to be determined from something outside ourselves and not from the strength within?

What truths do confident women possess that I can't seem to remember when it matters most?

Maybe it starts with looking our most painful flaws square in the eye.
I'm not size zero.
My body shows the effects of gravity, pregnancy, and, quite frankly, life.
I have thin, Scandinavian skin and

We Feel Pretty
(But It's Not an All-the-Time Gig)

Carleen: My hairdresser/sister/friend, Chloe, and I were talking about the feeling of losing yourself. She said she feels it sometimes—and it manifests in the problem of comparing yourself to people. She really made me think when she said, "You know, people use filters in their social media, but they're starting to use them in real life too! I see it every day." To me, that was a brilliant observation. We see these perfect images in the media, and we say that we want to be authentic, but then we construct and project this image that we have it ALL down. The hair, the nails, the family, the whatever . . . and if the people around you don't feel that, they experience some panic. Like, "Why am I not like that? Why can't I seem to be that put together?" I suppose that has always been around, but social media seems to give it a different twist these days. It's like we see it coming to life, and that messes with our ability to separate reality from a constructed image.

Lisa: Social media has absolutely magnified the filtered image of the perfect life. No one wants to be a Debbie Downer in terms of what they put out there, but I do appreciate it when people sometimes go 100 percent authentic. Like, this is me! Take it or leave it!

And then just a quick note about losing yourself: we have been focusing on middle-aged women because we ARE middle-aged women, but there are three men that I have talked to in the last week who basically said, "Um, hello—me too!" As adults, we have to attend to adulting, but why do we let our passions get pushed aside? I mean, there are the obvious things, but come on!

This was taken during the rough middle school years. It is one of my all time faves. (#Lili)

The "My Boy and Me" era—when I finally learned to be strong on my own. (#Lini)

hair.
I have a previously broken, bumpy nose.
I'm not a gymnast or a model or a muscle woman.

Maybe it continues by looking under those flaws to what's really bothering us.
There is a lot of trauma in my history.
My first marriage didn't work.
I've made a lot of mistakes.
I fear I will never be good enough.
I'm afraid I'll end up alone.

Maybe it continues when we stand up.
I have a lot to learn.
I have to take risks.
I have to execute a plan to change what is in my realm of influence.
I have to let go of the things I can't change.
I have to breathe.

Maybe as we stand up, we can allow ourselves to see the gifts in our lives.
I have a beautiful son.
I have a body that allows me to move, breathe, touch, and sleep.
I have a soul that lets me love, think, laugh, and forgive.
I have a great job that doesn't feel like one most of the time.
I have friends and family who know me and love me anyway.
I have passion.

Maybe we crank it up and move forward from a position of strength and determination, not of weakness and defeat.
I can be patient with myself.
I can forgive myself for having flaws.
I can take care of this body that houses my soul.
I can put down the baggage of my fractured past.
I can ask for help when I lose my perspective.
I can turn my back on the crazy media machine.
I can strive for balance.
I can find my inner spunk.
I can believe I am beautiful because I am perfect in my imperfection.
I can start again.

So I Married Me a Bear

Ten years ago, I was a hot mess. Not a dining room table that's got clutter on it. Not that bit of dust in the corner by the front door that needs to be picked up. Not even the inside of my car filled with morning commute breakfast/coffee/makeup, bags of merchandise that needs to be returned (one day), and stuff going to or from school that I'd been meaning to put away for three months.

Nope. I'm talking a H.O.T. mess. Picture everything that could possibly make you max out your homeowner's insurance policy. Flood. Fire. Earthquake. Tsunami. Tornado. Atomic Bomb. Alien Invasion. Killshot Solar Flare. I could call these things Acts of God, but I just can't go there. God wouldn't put me through what I went through. God loves me more than that.

It wasn't my divorce that made me a hot mess, even though a lot of people might assume that. While there was pain involved, it wasn't the soul-crushing experience many people go through. Matthew's dad and I decided that we made better friends than spouses, and leaving on good terms meant Matthew's life would be infinitely better. I guess you could say that as divorces and the reality of dual households go, we did okay. Everything has always been for The Boy™, after all.

It also wasn't the disastrous, short-term relationship I had next with an abusive narcissist that made me into a hot mess. Although it certainly was the proverbial straw that broke the camel's back. My spirit sank to a level of blackness I had never felt before. It made me afraid I would never feel the warmth of the sun again. I'd venture to say if I wasn't already a hot mess, that relationship wouldn't have happened. Neither would some of my other Major Missteps that I've had to forgive myself for before filing them under "Major Learning Experiences."

No, the roots of my Hot Messiness ran deep—all the way to my childhood and family of origin. I had people in my life who loved me deeply, yes—but there were seeds of dysfunction planted that grew into one of those invasive Weed Monsters you can't seem to kill, no matter how much you hack it, spray it with poison, or try to wish it away.

My particular Weed Monster is a hostile conglomeration of shame, loss, abandonment, and boundary violation. And, as happens when someone grows up in an emotional combat zone such as this (especially one no one else really knew about—or, worse, wanted to get involved with), I became a big ol' overly trusting empath. I was a peacemaker at all costs. A fixer. A people pleaser. An embarrassing oversharer. The owner of a broken compass. I was the

person who saw the good in everyone, even if everyone else saw rot. I gave and gave and gave until I had not a wisp of strength left. I made excuses for poor behavior and allowed people to mistreat me. I was an expert at self-flogging, even taking on guilt and responsibility that didn't belong to me. And I tried to rescue the souls of others who resembled people I had failed to rescue in the past, in hopes I would earn some sort of twisted redemption or crooked semblance of grace.

Scott walked into my life six weeks after an Atomic Bomb blew me to smithereens and put me in the aforementioned Twilight Zone. I had settled into the deepest, darkest corner of the bottom of a dried-up well—worn down, wrung out, and completely wasted away. And what about him—where was he? I'm positive he wasn't looking for a life partner, especially not one who had baggage like mine—which I cringingly told him about the first time we met.

That was not exactly the best way to start a new relationship.

But something about the other made us agree to see each other again (he likes to remind me he's the one who asked for my number, not the other way around). Something about the other made us decide to give a relationship a try. Something about the other made us choose to stay.

It wasn't easy at first. In fact, our first two years together were filled with lava-firestorm arguments; emotions that came upside down, inside out, and sideways out of our pores; as well as a record number of break-ups-and-get-back-togethers that would make even the worst celebrity relationship offenders blush. (He thinks I'm exaggerating here, but . . . no.)

The timing wasn't right to make a go of it those first two years because we both had too much healing to do. For all intents and purposes, our last break up (right before Thanksgiving, I might add) should have been the end of it. Done deal. Lick our wounds and move on. Chalk it up as another learning experience.

But it wasn't done, even though we both thought it was FOR SURE. We eventually found our way back to one another, but not until we had done some significant work to be better versions of ourselves. Not perfect, mind you, but better. We both realized that even though we were strong on our own, our lives were infinitely better with the other person. And yes, though we eventually took the leap and tied the knot under a big tree on a gorgeous day in July 2016, we made sure to take our sweet time so that the timing would be absolutely right.

Are we perfect? Are we each other's happy ever after? Was the day we got married the end

of everything painful and scary and irritating and maddening about Life, the Universe, and Everything? Were all our wounds healed? Are we finally living our fairy tale?

Nope. Far from it. That's reality, folks. That's marriage. We are two imperfect people choosing to live life together, for better and for worse and all the other things the traditional marriage vows say (except for "obey," right, honey?).

Sometimes our marriage resembles the firestorm it started out as.

There is a struggle between "I'm-too-tired-and-stressed-to-care-about-the-mess"-ness and "everything should be squared-away-why-can't-you-do-this-simple-thing"-ness (by now, you should be able to guess who fits each description).

We make mistakes.

We hurt each other sometimes.

We're insensitive.

We have to work to really hear the other person out, not just listen until it is our turn to speak.

I love this handsome, strong man so much. That right there is one of my favorite smiles. (#Lini)

We have the same damn arguments over and over. And over. Did I mention over again?

We drive each other batsh*t crazy sometimes.

The aging thing is a big drag for both of us, especially since I'm convinced he's going to have to put Alzheimer's Carleen in a home someday (just make sure it has a good hair salon and a coffee shop, baby).

But sometimes we are also the flip side of all those things.

We understand why the other person is messy or needs things to be tidy, and we give each other grace for being that way (at least for a little while ;)).

We try to do things for the other person that we know carry significant emotional meaning.

We know the other person almost better than they know themselves, and we work hard to say and do things in such a way that honors them.

We listen for the real story—the story underneath the story—the how and the why, the roots, and the ramifications. And if there is wisdom or revisioning to share, we share it, but only when the timing is right.

We make agreements to fight better (because fights happen). We call for and respect calls for time-outs when the emotion gets too intense to keep talking. We try to remember to reach out to touch one another to remind each other that we're real. We look into each other's eyes to recognize the hurt, not just see the frustration on the surface.

We take deep breaths when we need to, we hold our tongues when we can, and we celebrate what makes the other who they are.

We don't get bent out of shape about the other person's aging because we know that's part of the gig. And when the other person is bent out of shape about their age-related woes, we gently draw them in from the cold and back in front of the fire.

Above all, our marriage gives me hope, which comes in the form of the little things . . . and the big things.

It's how he holds me when we're falling asleep—even if we're crabby.

It's how he remembers stories from my childhood—like being too poor to get nice shoes—and then he buys me those exact shoes for Christmas.

It's how he will always change the air filter on my car, no matter how messy it is.

It's how he loves my son as if he were his own flesh and blood, even though being a step-parent is HARD.

It's how he sits next to me and watches plays and musicals, even though he'd much rather watch a UFC match. Or *The Shawshank Redemption* for the 100th time.

It's how he listens to my recounting of dreams and Pixie Dust experiences and says, "I'm glad that brought you the comfort you were looking for."

It's how he reminds me to be careful, to be mindful of my surroundings, and to give my trust only to those who have earned it.

It's how he knows about all my darkest moments but still sees me as light.

It's how he will never allow anyone to hurt me again so deeply that I feel like dying. They would have to come through him first.

It's how he reminds me of who I truly am when I, myself, have forgotten.

It's how he stays up late to get every bit of laundry done, even though we don't thank him enough. Ever.

It's how he honors my family, my heritage, and my need to be surrounded by the people I love in our home and at the lake.

It's how he reminds me my parents and brother are laughing in heaven, even though I feel like they are so far away.

It's how he gives me the space and freedom to be my own person, live my own life, and pursue creativity, which is my life force.

It's how he has freely given of himself to make Matthew and me feel like we finally have a home.

It's how he tolerates flamingos in the flower beds. Lots of flamingos.

It's in the gentle reality checks he gives me when I need them (even if I don't want them in the moment).

It's his laughter and storytelling when we get together with good friends.

It's his bedrock commitment to me and our relationship, even when I get anxious and start playing old tapes of self doubt that should have been wiped out when we chose to marry one another.

It's how he makes enough coffee in the morning for me to have some too, even when I'm on summer vacation and he has to work.

My husband is a man of action, protection, and strength, and he GETS me, even—and especially—when I'm being Little Me.

And I do the same for him.

Marriage is hard work, no doubt. But we show up for it.

And make coffee.

Chapter Nineteen

YOUR TURN!

Take some time to write about Getting Up from one of life's falls. You might want to use some of the prompts below or go your own direction. Do what feels natural and right for you and listen to what your writing tells you about yourself and your life.

- Tell about a time when you tried to get back on your skis before you were ready/centered. What happened?

- Tell about a time when someone tried to force you to get on your skis before you were ready/centered. What happened?

- How much space do you have in your life to reset and center yourself?

- How comfortable are you setting boundaries for yourself, so you can reset and center? How comfortable are you asking for what you need?

- What strength of yours plays the biggest role in helping you stand up again when you need to? What gets in the way?

- Who are the people who stand with you and help you? What do they do for you?

- When have you helped others? Or, when could you help others in the future? What was that like/what could that be like for you?

- My biggest "a-ha" related to this section is . . . because . . .

- I hope to . . .

- I am grateful for . . .

Chapter Twenty

#SPINGOLD: YOU GOT THIS, GIRL

Idea #1: Map Out Your Balance

Sometimes the one thing we need to get up and try again is a #GentleLlamaKick that comes in the form of awareness. Every single one of us gets off balance, and the reasons why are as plentiful as the grains of sand on the beach. Maybe you really LIKE physical exercise but detest doing finances. Guess which one gets more of your attention? Or maybe you have struggled with relationships in the past but have found success at work, so it's not surprising you gravitate to where you feel most appreciated.

Whatever you story is, we want you to chew on this: to keep your bus moving forward, you've gotta have good tires.

There are lots of ways to view balance in our lives, but one we like in particular is Oola (which is different from Oula, our favorite dance fitness class). Troy Amdahl and Dave Braun, who are affectionately known as the Oola Guys, came up with the concept of Oola after a particularly challenging time in life. They realized if you give equal time to seven key areas, you will feel better, which will allow you to be a better human in the world. To make it easier for us to remember the seven parts of Oola, they made them all start with the letter "F":

- Family

- Friends

- Fitness

- Finances

Rule #4

- Field (job)

- Fun

- Faith

You can read all their thoughts, stories, and suggestions in their book, *Oola: Find Balance in an Unbalanced World,* and you can also poke around their website at www.oolalife.com. For our purposes here, we'll use the list of F words (heh—and you thought there was only one).

Let's consider how the Fs are functioning in your life and in relation to one other. It's time to get out your special markers! (Pssst! You can do a version of this on their website, too—just look for the Oola Wheel.)

1. On a piece of paper or on a page in your journal, write "Oola" in the center and circle it. This is the hub of your wheel.

2. Give yourself a "gut" score for each F word (one to ten, one is low and ten is high) based on how healthy you think you are. Don't overthink it—listen to your intuition. You can be completely honest because no one needs to see what you write. Things you might consider about each area could be:

    a. The amount of time you devote to it
    b. How healthy your attitude is toward it
    c. How much it enhances your life or detracts from your life
    d. How it affects your loved ones, positively or negatively
    e. The habits you have in relation to it, healthy or unhealthy
    f. Whether it brings you joy or causes you stress—and why

3. Give your wheel some spokes. Write each of the seven F Words on the paper and connect them to "Oola" in the center. The length of each spoke should roughly correspond to the number you assigned it—so a seven spoke would be longer than a three spoke.

4. Make a "tire" by connecting the Fs.

Now, step back and look at your wheel. Would it roll down a hill smoothly, or would it galumph along like a car driving through mashed potatoes? Are there some parts of your wheel that are completely throwing your bus off-balance? Could you reallocate some of your energy from one section to others that aren't as robust? What parts of your wheel need a boost? Are there certain spokes that are longer for reasons you can't control? Do you see them evening

out later—so maybe now is a good time to extend yourself some grace? Do you need help lengthening a certain spoke?

Keep in mind you don't have to have all of your spokes at a "ten" in order to be balanced. Your wheel can roll along just fine with equal spokes of six or three (and that just shows you there's room to grow, right?). Also remember your spokes will grow and shrink at different times in your life, and that's totally fine.

Finally, it's important to remember that you can't keep your wheel perfectly round all the time. Nobody can! But there is great benefit to being aware of how your wheel is rolling so you know what kind of help to seek and adjustments to make along the way. Above all, you've got to drive your own bus, Sister!

#Mood (#Lili)

We Can't Even

Carleen: Can dry shampoo fix this, or do I need booze?

Lisa: Two words: Struggle Bus. Beep beep!

Mexican Coke in a bottle—when you just can't deal. #AllTheThings (#Lini)

Idea #2: Dreamboard It

Dreamboarding . . . ahhh. Doesn't it make you feel better to just say that word aloud in your head? Dreamboarding. YAAAASSSS, child. Breathe it in. Inhale . . . and exhale.

This idea isn't new—it's all over Pinterest, it's a favorite activity of life coaches, and you can read about it in a zillion different blogs and articles online. I (Lisa) learned about it for the first time in a multi-level marketing business. That company didn't fit my style, but learning to

Dreamboard was my takeaway. What is it, exactly? Is there a right way to do it? And what if you just don't have time and energy to get all crafty with the decoupage?

(Okay, sisters from the 1970s . . . we know at some point in your life, you probably cut out a picture of Holly Hobbie or the Critter Sitters, put it on a piece of wood, and decoupaged it. Wait . . . not everyone did that? Or maybe you're just a bit too young to have this experience? All right, then...we're feeling a MAKE AND TAKE coming on!)

The central idea behind Dreamboarding is to create a representation of what you want your life to look like. There is great power in collecting words and images on a board before placing it in a place where you can see it regularly. Use it as a reminder of why you work so hard or why you need to keep moving forward when things get tough.

Your board can be as simple or as complicated as you'd like it to be—there are no cosmic extra credit points for decoupage (but we totally encourage you to try it sometime #BecauseDecoupage). There's also no hard and fast rule that says you have to make it fancy or massive or decked out with bling from your local craft store.

If you don't want to spend the time making a physical board out of glue, magazines, tagboard, and stickers, you can do it digitally. Isn't that the brilliance of Pinterest boards? You could also create a digital image to keep on your phone's lock screen. Or print it out and hang it where you'll frequently see it. You could also kick it old school and draw. Whatever medium floats your boat is what you should do—don't worry about what other people do. Flowers don't compare themselves—they just bloom!

Some Variations on the Dreamboard Idea:

1. As a positive part of your life comes together, document the journey and/or your growth on a board! Carleen did this when she planned her bonus wedding—it helped her enjoy the experience more to see it gelling, and it also helped her see what needed more attention.

2. Make your Dreamboard an intention board—as in, use it to visualize what you want to manifest in your life. This may feel a little #PixieDusty to some of you, but there's actually #BecauseScience behind this angle (think about the Olympic athletes who are coached to visualize themselves succeeding and winning). If it feels better to call it a Prayer Board, that's totally cool too. Whatever works for you and your belief system is just right.

3. Don't feel you have to include every part of your life on your Dreamboard. You can zero in on one area of life at a time, like work, relationships, fitness, or dessert. Just listen to the still, small voice inside you to see what she has to say.

4. Most Dreamboards are kept out in the open where you can see them, but you could also tuck yours away, like a time capsule. You can dig it out later to see what came to pass and what is still in progress.

5. Dreamboards make great journaling prompts, so if you are the writing type, use those images to jump-start a piece of dream-focused writing. This may help you further clarify what it all means!

Idea #3: Move Your Body

As a Woman in the Middle, there is no getting around the fact your body is different now than it was when you were in your teens and twenties. Thank you, Captain Obvious, for making another appearance. "Different" does not have to equal "bad," however!

It's time to throw such a limiting attitude out, Girlfriends (right along with the idea that you can't wear a trend the next time it comes back into fashion, like rainbow shirts and huarache sandals). It's no secret that pop culture, marketing, and the whole retail industry have done damage to women (and men!) by suggesting that being young is EVERYTHING. Let's be revolutionary and not validate that false idea! Youth is great—don't get us wrong—but it is NOT more valuable than other ages. To believe otherwise is to discount and devalue most of our lifespan and one of the greatest gifts we've been given—a body to carry our soul while it moves and experiences life.

Because we want to practice what we babble about, we embarked on a mission to get ourselves moving again. We did things like running, power yoga, Oula dance fitness, kayaking, and hiking. In the process of having a ton of fun and improving our health, we had a few a-ha moments we'd like to share to encourage you to get out and wiggle your butt. Is this an exhaustive list? Nope. But it's a start!

1. Incorporating movement in your life can interrupt patterns. You could sit on the couch and watch cat videos . . . or you could walk on the treadmill and watch cat videos. You could explore half a package of chocolate chips because you're bored . . . or you could explore someplace interesting, like a hiking trail. You could sit and spin on an irratio-

nal thought that raises your cortisol levels, or you could sit and spin on a bike.

You don't have to jump right to Crossfit, Sisters. You can, but you don't have to. Be okay with the fact it may take you some time to get back into working out. Start where you are. You are a badass just by being alive. Believe it.

2. Trying something new can be refreshing, and even if you totally suck at it, the #LaughFactor can totally be enough to make it worth the experience. Who cares if you don't do it right or look a little silly? Everyone there is focusing on themselves, not you. And even if they do notice you're a newbie, nine times out of ten, they'll admire the fact you got up and tried. If nothing else comes out of it, think of the story you'll have to tell. It's a win-win, Sisters.

This was back when Brett Favre was a Viking and Matthew and I became fans of the hometown team, thanks to Scott teaching us the basics of the game. Matthew could use the #KidCard. My lame excuse was that I was a Band Noogie and spent my time talking on the bleachers between songs! (#Lini)

3. Moving your body can make you feel less stuck and more present in the moment. We women often get ourselves tangled up in #AllTheThings and become #TheGlue for everyone else. We also spend a lot of time focusing on the past or our shortcomings—our hurts, mistakes, failed relationships—until we become #Unglued. Our bodies might even hold on to the emotional remnants of past trauma and cause us physical pain. Any number of things can keep us from the life we're living and the direction in which we're going. We can even feel totally paralyzed.

Girlfriends, we were created for so much more than that. Physical movement allows us to feel our bodies move through space and our breath move in and out of our lungs. It also allows us to see the results of our actions in the now.

Family trip out to the apple orchard. It was such a beautiful day. (#Lili)

4. Getting out and moving can help you feel more connected to others. As we talked about in the Find Your Team Strategy, a partner or team can be an incredible source of encouragement and inspiration, as long as they are "your people," support you, and have your best interests in mind. Go for a walk with a friend or coworker and chat it up! Try a group fitness class! Find an online forum of people who share your movement passions! You don't have to go it alone, Sisters, and think of all you can learn from the people around you.

5. Movement in your body can inspire momentum in other parts of your life. Moving more made us want to do other things that were good for us, too, like eating veggies and meat instead of ice cream for a meal (okay, ice cream for dinner won't kill you, but it shouldn't become a habit). Trying a new activity might boost your confidence and lead you to think, "Hey, I did X activity . . . what if I did Y? That could be fun!" Whatever positives you gain, we bet as you begin feeling better, you will want to do what you can to maintain forward motion.

While it's true that moving your body after a hiatus (or if you've never done it) can be intimidating, it can also help you in countless ways—and you deserve every one of them, Soul Sisters. You may just have to do things another way to get where you want to go. As Carleen's friend Karla used to say, "You just have to find a way to wiggle."

Who's up for an adventure? WE ARE!

(Stay tuned to www.getupandtryagain.com for more on our #EXTRAOrdinary Adventures!)

Idea #4: Oils We Like for This

Peppermint
Lemon
Orange
Lime
Grapefruit
Lemon Myrtle
Ylang Ylang
Rosemary
Black Pepper
Ginger
Cinnamon

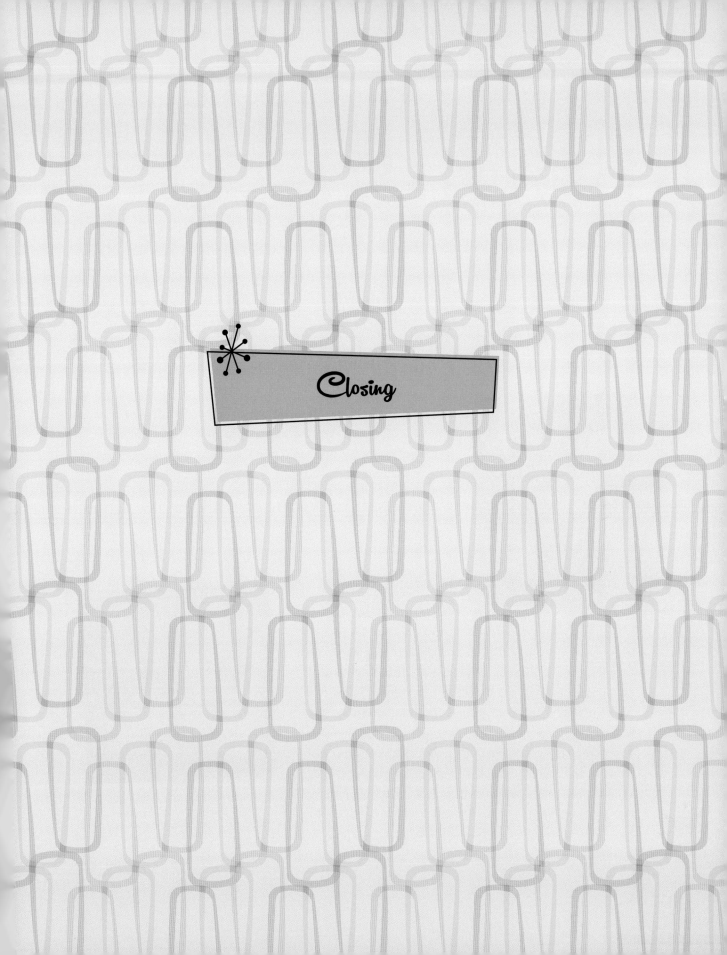

Closing

A FANTASTIC DAY ON THE LAKE

Dear Lovelies,

It's been a fantastic day on the lake. The sun is going down, and we can tell it's going to be an incredible sunset. The boat has been docked. The life jackets are tucked away, and our kick-ass swimsuits and wet towels are drying on the line out back. It's time to make the campfire and get the Tonka supplies. We arrange the camp chairs to allow our conversations to ooze and blend like melty chocolate and marshmallows inside a s'more.

Wherever my dad is playing the guitar will always be my happy place! (#Lili)

We stand at the edge of the water and let it buss our toes like a mother kissing her lake-happy kidlets goodnight before they crawl into their sleeping bags to relive the day's adventures in their dreams. Dad plays John Denver on his six-string in the background. The sky whispers, "Do you have your sweatshirt? Did you get a cold drink? Are you comfortable and happy? Good! Settle in—the last show of the night is about to begin. I know you THINK you've seen beautiful sunsets before, but wait 'til you see what we have in store for you tonight. It's going to #EXTRAAuroraBorealisINCREDIBLE."

Lake Vermilion will always be a sanctuary to me—the place where I can feel the spirits of my ancestors in the sand. When I lived at home (just fifteen minutes away from it), I used to drive there on particularly stressful days and just sit on that beach and breathe. (#Lini)

Ahhhhhhhhhhhh. Can you feel it?

Okay, sisters . . . we've saved the best for last. It's time to pull out all the stops and lay down the ONE IDEA that we hope you'll take away from this crazy #EXTRAOrdinary Endeavor of ours. We placed it here for a reason: it's truly what we see as the key to Life, the Universe, and Everything (to borrow a phrase from writer Douglas Adams—one of Big Brother Cedric's favorites).

At the heart and soul of it all, we ask you to take a good, long look at what inspires and guides you:

Is it love, or is it fear?

Girlfriends, everything—absolutely EVERYTHING—rests on how you answer this question.

Love connects, rejuvenates, comforts, encourages, accepts, builds, inspires, and unites. Fear disconnects, kills, ridicules, discourages, rejects, tears down, defeats, and separates. We know which one feels better and which one feels worse. We know which one makes us soar to new heights and which one shoots us out of the sky. We know which one emboldens us to respectfully challenge the behaviors of others and which one causes us to allow injustice. We know which one makes the world better . . . and which one tears it—and us—apart.

We know. We SO know—every single last one of us.

The time has come for you to step out of the darkness and into the light. Fear has gotten us nowhere good. It has stolen some of our best moments and experiences. It has broken our relationships and made us do ugly-ish things. Let's believe in our hearts that we can do better.

It's time to reset your compass.

Believe it or not, this is a firework going off. I took it as a sign. (#Lini)

Each of us comes equipped with a standard internal guidance system. Call it your personal GPS, your gut, your intuition, your spirit guide, the still, small voice—call it whatever you want to or need to. We're going to call it the Compass.

If you think back to what you learned as a kid at camp or in science class, you might remember that compasses align themselves with the magnetic field of the earth. The compass is one of the oldest, most trusted tools of navigation in history, and without it, sailors would have completely lost their way on many a sea voyage.

Compasses are not immune from influence, however. Electromagnetic fields, especially those coming from other magnets, can affect the accuracy of a compass—and if those fields are moving (or if there are several of them around your compass at the same time), the needle on a compass will actually spin and provide unusable data.

That's what fear does—it messes with your compass and gets you completely off course, especially if you have it coming at you from all sides. When it starts spinning out of control, you must move away from whatever or whomever is giving you bad data. You will know when your compass is working correctly again, however. You will feel it in your gut. The trick is to trust your intuition.

Love is our North, sisters, because it lives within each of us and always has. If you move away from fear, your needle will settle down, and you will find your way home.

Lead with love, even if the only person you lead is yourself.

Now, we're not going to lie—moving through painful experiences takes time, energy, support, determination, and a whole lot of faith. And since life is circular, you WILL come face-to-face with your pain more than once, and you WILL have to weather more storms.

But Sisters, every journey back to center starts with a single step toward the right thing. And that step can be as easy as flipping your attitude about what's happening to you instead of wallowing in your pain or blaming someone else. Remember, you are the one thing in life you can control (Lin-Manuel Miranda, thank you for your #WordMagic!). You alone can own your stories, recognize their lessons, and begin your healing process.

So, move away from fear and toward love—for yourself, for others, and for the world. Ask for help. And remember, sugarcoating a turd is a valuable skill, and your brain will believe anything you tell it . . . so why not err on the side of optimism and nurture some positive energy? Here's what that process could look like using some familiar negative self-talk phrases:

We Say . . .	Instead, We Could Say . . .
"I hate my cellulite."	"I have legs to carry me around on grand adventures."
"This person doesn't make me happy."	"The only person responsible for my happiness is me."
"I did something bad in the past."	"I am not the person I was then. I am stronger."
"That person is a jerk."	"That person might be dealing with something I know nothing about, and if it were me, I would appreciate grace and kindness. But it's also okay to protect myself."
"All we humans do is hurt each other."	"There are helpers everywhere, and I can be one, too."
"The world is falling apart."	"There are things we can do to help our world heal."
"I'm falling apart."	"Something is nudging me to grow."
"I'm too sensitive."	"My sensitivity is a great tool because it helps me understand others. I just need to be careful not to absorb their stuff."
"I screwed that up."	"I can learn from this experience and get up and try again."

On the surface, this practice may seem simplistic, and not everyone defaults to optimism (like we do). We also recognize that sometimes we just need to look our pain full in the face and sit with it. That's okay—just don't sit with it forever. Don't let it run in your veins. Don't let it define you. Don't fall in step with the rhythm of negativity. Don't allow it to turn you into a shadow of your former self. Instead—find the lesson, reset your compass, and start again. Taking one step at a time counts as forward movement.

Just remember what you learned about building a fire when you were a kid. Put the kindling down first and build a tent around it with the little sticks. Strike the match—now, light it in at least three spots to give it a good chance to get going. Did it catch? Great! Add a few

little-bit-bigger sticks and gently blow on it—make sure you are feeding that baby flame the right amount of what it needs to keep burning. Keep an eye on it . . . watch it carefully . . . listen to it tell you when to start laying bigger pieces of wood until you have a steady, sustained fire.

Well, Sisters, the Great Big Book-Writing Adventure is coming to a close. We hope we have been an oasis in your desert. We hope we have fanned a spark that will become a big flame. We hope we have created a welcoming space in which you can think, dream, learn, love, and make #EXTRAOrdinary plans for your beautiful life!

We also hope you will take action on those plans and share your #EXTRA with others! What happens to one of us affects the rest of us, so fan those beautiful butterfly wings. Your #EXTRA has the power to warm your face, fill your ears with happy, crackling songs, and light up a world in need of healing. You possess the most beautiful pair of ruby slippers imaginable, and they've been there all along.

Carleen: Hey, #Lili. Before we go, I feel like we should end with one more #PingyPingPingSession because that's how we roll. Sound good? Squeee?

Lisa: SQUEEEEEEEE!!! Sisters, we want you to discover, uncover, rediscover, and reacquaint yourself with your Crazy-Awesome, Messy-Hearted-Woman Self. Create your own destiny, design your own life, set your own rules, delineate your boundaries, and be #EXTRA. Don't waste any more time NOT being #EXTRA. Shine like a diamond and define yourself. No one else gets to do that—not society, not others outside of you, and CERTAINLY not Fear. You! So, remember who you are and then #PleaseTellYourStory! YOU are strong, you are beautiful, you are badass, and you have something to SAY!

Carleen: Yaaaaaasssss! We have a moral imperative to erase our invisibility, girlfriends, so let yourself be seen.

Don't worry about what others think. The people who will love you for you WILL come into your life at the right time. Focus your energy on loving yourself—protect, heal, and care for your Little Me because she needs you! That love will spill over onto others—it can't help itself. Become part of the #HealingLoveTeam that our world so desperately needs

Lisa: Who are the stakeholders here? WE are! WE must disrupt and design to make this a better world. WE can change the status quo. WE can break the chains of fear with love, resilience, and collective efficacy. Even if things get uncomfortable, ambiguous, and downright challenging, the end result will be well worth it. If now is not your time, then when?

Carleen: As our friend Elizabeth Claeys said, "Everyone has a purpose and a right to joy. We never know how long we get in this life to find our purpose and experience joy. It's never too early, or late, to go for it." With our team, it is not boots on the ground—it is skis on the water. Are you ready?

Lisa: GO (TEAM, GO)!!!!!!!!

> **You are love, Sisters.**
> **You are #EXTRAOrdinary.**
> **And together, we are unstoppable.**

(Psssst! It only takes a spark! Pass it on!)

We Are #SoulSister Fangirls

So we have some #SOULSISTERS out there (besides YOU and Brené and Liz and Glennon) . . . people we hear about and think, "YASSS! We know your souls, Starshines!!" They're our besties—they just don't know it yet. #ShoutOut to . . .

El Gato Gomez: She is an AH-MA-ZING, badass midcentury artist! We're TOTALLY skiing on the same lake! She is painting our SOULS. We LOVE us some El Gato (and this is why we call our publisher #AmyGato)! And our editor—#RhiaPusheen!! We love us some #KittyKatRP!

Lauren Ostrowski Fenton: Her voice is BUT-TAH. You will feel like your best self when you listen to her meditations (you on vacation on a beach, sipping a fou-fou cocktail). We listen to her and think, "How does she KNOOOW?" Check her out on YouTube!

Ruth Bader Ginsberg: The Notorious R.B.G. #BecauseDissentCollar. Word. That is all.

Michelle Obama . . . #SWOON. That is also all. #MichelleGoals

Used with permission by El Gato Gomez

#GLORIOUS GLOSSARY

Midwinter writing. It gets cold in my office! (#Lili)

Okay, look . . . we use a lot of #Hashtags.

Yep, we know. Lots of people find them irritating, especially if they are overused (like when your elementary school kiddo keeps telling the same joke over and over again, and you have to tell them, "Honey, one time is hilarious, two times is funny, three times is annoying . . . four times is . . . hey, look over there! Is that a polar bear?")

#However . . .

Used in moderation, hashtags can be just the emphasis we're looking for when we're writing or texting back and forth. And then they morph. And then they take on new meaning. Yaaaaassss.

So here are a few of ours. They aren't all in the book, but that's what makes them . . . extra #EXTRA. There's room for you to add your own.

Snug as a bug in a rug . . . with coffee. (#Lini)

#EXTRA	True love. Vibes. That sparkly spark of something-something that makes you you and has been there from the beginning of time . . . and to hell with anyone who thinks you're silly. See also #RubySlippers.
#RubySlippers	The realization that you've "had it [love/#EXTRA] all along," à la Dorothy in The Wizard of Oz.
#EXTRAOrdinary	All of us . . . us, you, we. We are just regular, ordinary people who possess something-something special. We just do, and when we recognize it in each other, we SQUEEEEEEEE! See also #SQUEEEEEEEEEEEEEE.
#SQUEEEEEEEEEEEEEE	What one might say when one feels extreme childlike delight; a Lisa-ism. Must contain several or unlimited number of E's.
#SQUEEE?	This SQUEEE contains only three E's and is used exclusively as a question. The question is whether or not a given thing is SQUEEE-able.
#Flamingolicious	Yaaaassss
#Llamicles	Pieces of our hearts that have been scattered, usually without our permission; it's totally okay if they haven't made it home yet (they will). Origin: Lisa found a pink llama duster to sweep up . . . particles. So naturally, this morphed into #Llamicles.
#SubAtomicLlamicles	A further clarification of #Llamicles.
#OOOOChild	A big ol' cleansing breath when we're about to lose our minds.
#AtomicLlamas	This is the animal manifestation of our pieces and parts coming back together into something amazingly awesome. What about #SpaceLlamas? See also #SpaceLlamas.
#SpaceLlamas	Lisa found a patch with them on it. We think it was a sign.

#MichelleGoals — Because we love Michelle Obama. #NuffSaid

#NuffSaid — That's all we've got to say about that!

#Karma — The joke's on you . . . or someone else who deserves it because they were sh*tty.

#ReclaimYourLlamicles — Find the scattered pieces of yourself . . . and know it's not done yet . . . and might never be done . . . but that's okay because we are currently experiencing what you're currently experiencing . . . so we're kinda in a club! See also #Mercury.

#Mercury — That shiny silver stuff that beautifully OOZES BACK TOGETHER . . . you know the stuff! (#BecauseScience) See also #BecauseScience.

#BecauseScience — Look, we are ordinary people. We aren't scientists. We aren't social scientists. We're just . . . us. But we know that there's great science out there, and we love it . . . #BecauseScience

#BecauseThatsHowLifeWorks — Just lean into it. Things don't always make sense. Or they don't now, but will later. Or maybe not. Whatever. See also #AcceptTheCrazy.

#AcceptTheCrazy — Just do it. It won't hurt. Much. We promise.

#Clicking — It's happening, people . . . the flow is here . . . the lens fits on the camera!

#SilverLining — Unapologetic optimism from which we suffer (hey, it gets us through the bad times). See also #Rainbow, #PotOfGold, and #Oasis.

#Rainbow — All the colors . . . and our LGBTQIA sweeties. We love you all.

#PotOfGold	What's waiting for us after the sh*tstorm clears . . . because the Universe has things in mind we don't know about.
#Oasis	When you're in the desert, look for the oasis . . . we have cocktails.
#SwirlingSubatomicParticles	So, two Missouri Synod Lutherans walk into a junior high building, but it takes them eighteen years to really FIND each other! See also #SwirlyGirls.
#SwirlyGirls	The two of us living our lives made crazy by #AllTheThings. See also #AllTheThings.
#AllTheThings	The sh*tload of stuff we women need to deal with (and because we're women, we don't need to list them off because we already KNOOOOOOOOOOOOOW what they are).
#AllTheAges	Inspired by "Eleven," by Sandra Cisneros. You are not just the age you are . . . nay-nay. You are every one of the years you've been, "like pennies in a tin Band-Aid box," as she puts it.
#Percolating	Taking your time to observe and think before acting.
#Percolators	People who have the tendency to percolate.
#Carbonation	Jumping in and running with something; figuring it out as you go because you just gotta run with it and see what happens.
#PopPop	The sound you hear in your soul when you CARBONATE.
#Camping	Sitting on the deck, writing! Someday, we'll be #Glamping! See also #Glamping.

#Glamping Roaming around the country in a vintage travel trailer that's all decked out with flamingos, llamas, and all things retro pink/yellow/turquoise; our retirement plan. For now, another name for #Camping.

#TheCities The Twin Cities—Minneapolis and/or St. Paul.

#CosmicDJ When the universe somehow knows which music you need to hear; see also #LilMingo and #DJJazzyLlama.

#LilMingo Carleen's music alter ego.

#DJJazzyLlama Lisa's music alter ego.

#WWCS Waterskiing Women of a Certain Season. It could also mean, What Would Cedric Say? :)

#Doink What you call someone who does exactly the opposite of what you need.

#Pinging When you click with another human and the ideas ping back and forth like the ball in a pinball machine.

#PleaseTellYourStory A riff on "Who lives, who dies, who tells your story?" from the #EXTRAIncredible show *Hamilton* by our #SoulBrother, Lin-Manuel Miranda. Your story matters—please share it with the world!

#kk Okay okay. Variation: KK! (Use this when you are excited.)

#LlamicleCake The dessert you have while celebrating the successful herding of at least some of your llamicles.

#SpinGold Grow from a rotten situation and/or focus on love.

#WhiskeyDiscussion An honest, heartfelt conversation that happens after a shot of Jameson (and just one; that's all we need).

Bonus #2

PARALLEL LIVES

As we dug through our picture boxes and shared stories, we realized that we have led parallel lives (which is both cool and a little spooky). There are a few of them sprinkled throughout the book, but we thought we'd share a few more of our favorites because, well, we're family, right? The experience of seeing our parallels taught us that even though we are unique, we truly are more alike than different. And so it is with all people. #AllOnTheSameTeam

I look sugar high and I hadn't even dug in yet. Maybe I was taking a moment of blissful silence. (#Lili)

I still get that look on my face when someone puts a cake in front of me. (#Lini)

I felt so grown up in this dress! I had a wonderful evening at Homecoming '88. (#Lili)

This was one of my grad pictures. Check out the line from my inside-out nylons on my belly. #NoPhotoshopBackThen (#Lini)

Our band was really, really good! Go Magi! I am glad that we didn't have to wear our golden, fuzzy Marge Simpson hats at the ND State Fair Parade in July! (#Lili)

The Virginia Marching Blues were the BEST! Band Buddy Nichole (I call her "Heco") is right behind me and my piccolo. We often sang "God Bless America" instead of playing it. (#Lini)

My sister and me catching the rays and listening to the boom box on a hot Lake Vermilion afternoon. And I thought I was chubby! I've got a Diet Coke and M&Ms in there somewhere. They canceled each other out! (#Lini)

Best rays around! I think that there are probably a radio, sunflower seeds, and a Diet Coke behind me. (#Lili)

I think that 1989 was probably the zenith of my huge hair. (#Lili)

My bestie Laura and I show off our awesome '80s style at a "non prom" (no evil rock and roll). I'm wearing my favorite red bow shoes! (#Lini)

This was such a wonderful day! I felt like a princess in all that handmade beautiful floof! (#Lili)

This was the first time my dad ever wore a tux. He kept me calm by making me laugh (equally hard on the mascara as crying, however). (#Lini)

The Last Word

#EXTRAORDINARY ACKNOWLEDGMENTS

We have so many #EXTRAOrdinary people to thank for the love and support they've given us as we've chased after our dream of writing a book.

To our husbands, Kris and Scott—you have been our steadfast rocks. Thank you for being great sounding boards, saying "sure" to a few more Chipotle/Leeann Chin nights than usual, and rolling with it whenever we announce that we have yet another crazy idea. We love you like crazy. #TimingIsEverything (#Lini) #ThirdTimesTheCharm (#Lili)

To our kiddos, Lauren and Matthew—you have been our best cheerleaders. Thank you for providing your honest opinions, reminding us what authenticity is all about, and being open to spontaneous adventures. We Mama Bears love you fiercely and forever.

To our sisters, our mothers, our aunties Donna and Tammy, and our girlfriends—you have been our models of grace and fire. Thank you for loving us unconditionally and showing us what it means to be strong and spunky. We want to be just like you when we grow up.

To our brothers, our fathers, Uncle Vern, and our guy friends (we couldn't leave you out, now could we?)—what we said about our sisters, mothers, aunties, and girlfriends applies to you guys too. We're all about the equality thing. ;)

To Trevor Church, Amy Miller, and Beth Ocar—you have been our nudgers. Thank you for planting the seeds of this project by telling us we had a book in us and encouraging us every step of the way. We appreciate you tremendously.

To our publisher, #AmyGato at Wise Ink Creative Publishing—you have been our dreamweav-

er. Thank you for believing in us from our first cheeky message and supporting us as the waves rolled up and down throughout this process. We have called you "our publisher" from Day One.

To our editor, #RhiaPusheen—you have been our sunshine. Thank you for helping us sing more clearly and affirming that what we had to say was important and necessary. We look forward to many more #PixieDust moments with you.

To our graphic designers, #Athena and #KiMAGIC—you have been our interpreters. Thank you for making the spirit of #EXTRAOrdinary come to life with your artistic talents and patiently putting up with our fingers in #AllThePies. You transformed our work into a real book. We are in awe of you.

To our counselors and therapists, past and present—you have been our life preservers. Thank you for helping us figure out what to keep and what to toss when it comes to feelings and stuff. By helping us, you've helped us help others. ¡¡¡Muchas gracias para siempreeeeeee!!!

To all our loves on the Other Side—you have been our inspiration. Thank you for putting whispers in our ears and memories in our heads exactly when we needed them most. We hope we have made you proud. Cedric, without you and your metaphor, we wouldn't have a book. We are honored to be your voice so everyone in the world knows what a beautiful genius you are (yes, that's a present tense verb—because you are still with us, Big Brother).

To all the #EXTRAOrdinary Women out there—you have been the fire in our belly. Thank you for being exactly who you are. We can't wait to see what fun is going to pop up for the #EXTRAOrdinary Teamy-Team-Team next.

Closing

BIBLIOGRAPHY

1. Borge, John. *Counseling—Pastor Carl Lee.* 1989, Concordia College Archives, Moorhead, Minnesota.

2. Elsesser, Kim. *Power Posing is Back: Amy Cuddy Successfully Refutes Criticism.* April 3, 2018. https://www.forbes.com/sites/kimelsesser/2018/04/03/power-posing-is-back-amy-cuddy-successfully-refutes-criticism/#5ac268a73b8e

3. Pet-Assisted Visitation Volunteer Services. http://www.pawsforpeople.org/

4. Rovner, Julie. *Pet Therapy: How Animals And Humans Heal Each Other.* March 5, 2012. https://www.npr.org/sections/health-shots/2012/03/09/146583986/pet-therapy-how-animals-and-humans-heal-each-other.

5. Unknown. *Retropedia - A Look at Style and Design Through Time.* January 23, 2013. http://revivalvintagestudio.blogspot.com/2013/01/mid-century-design-in-atomic-age-beauty.html

6. Weil, Andrew, M.D. *Is There Anything to "Earthing"?.* January 8, 2018. https://www.drweil.com/health-wellness/balanced-living/healthy-living/is-there-anything-to-earthing/

About the Authors

CARLEEN MATTS-BEHRENDS

Carleen Matts-Behrends has been a junior high English teacher for twenty-five years, which means she has written loads of five-paragraph essays, pages of curriculum, and countless personal narratives (a few of the latter have been published on Facebook for her five adoring fans). She told her then-boyfriend, now-husband Scott she was going to write a book someday, and she finally made good on her promise. She loves flamingos, cake, mashed potatoes, and English Springer Spaniels (but she lives in town now that she's a grown-up, so no, she doesn't have one—yet). She can't get enough of the outdoors, whether it's on a trail somewhere or in her flower beds. She dreams of traveling the country in a glamper and visiting every major league baseball park with her son, Matthew. Also, she makes the best chocolate chip cookies ever. Carleen got her B.A. in English Education at Concordia College and her Master's Degree in Education at St. Mary's University of Minnesota. She is in the forty-second grade.

LISA SHAFFNER SOHN

Lisa Shaffner Sohn has been a high school Spanish teacher for twenty-seven years . . . except for that one year she randomly worked for Wells Fargo Retirement Plan Services and gave benefits enrollment meetings and investment updates in English and Spanish across the country. So there was that. She has one husband, one daughter, two dogs, and a cat. She loves llamas, tacos, traveling, and cake. Someday she will live by the ocean, where she will collect rocks and jog daily on the shore. She also makes a damn good holiday turkey! Lisa got her B.S. in Spanish and in Education from Minot State University, and her Master's in Education from Hamline University. She is in the forty-fourth grade.